WRESTLING
with
REALITY

WRESTLING
with
REALITY

Martin Weber

Pacific Press Publishing Association
Boise, Idaho
Oshawa, Ontario, Canada

Edited by B. Russell Holt
Designed by Dennis Ferree
Cover art by Giraudon/Art Resource, New York
         Eugene Delacroix, "Jacob and the Angel"
Typeset in 10/12 Century Schoolbook

Unless otherwise indicated, all Scripture references are from
the New King James Version.

The author assumes full responsibility for the accuracy of all
facts and quotations cited in this book.

Library of Congress Cataloging-in-Publication Data:
Weber, Martin, 1951-
    Wrestling with reality / Martin Weber.
         p.   cm.
    ISBN 0-8163-1153-6
    1. Church and social problems—Seventh-Day Adventist. 2.
Seventh-Day Adventists—Doctrines. I. Title.
HN37.S48W42   1993
261.8'08'8267—dc20   92-44880
                                                          CIP

93 94 95 96 97 ● 5 4 3 2

Dedication

To J. David Newman—
my senior editor at *Ministry*
magazine. He is also my
friend and my brother.

Contents

Introduction

(Keeping a balance)

Everyone in the room was going to die, and they knew it. I was attending a support group for people with terminal illnesses. They sat in a circle and told their stories. One of the men announced that he had AIDS. A sudden sense of awe fell upon the others. Although this man was in the same situation as everyone else there, he became an instant celebrity. Why? Because his was the only disease that Hollywood honors as politically correct.

AIDS is a horrible way to die, but so are cancer and a host of other fatal illnesses that kill far more people. Medical research is sorely needed in all of them. Yet the government is spending ten times as much on AIDS as on other leading diseases *combined*. Is the homosexual lobby appreciative?

No. As if their own moral behavior had nothing whatever to do with the disease, homosexuals actually accused the Reagan and Bush administrations of killing people with AIDS because *more* money hadn't been devoted toward AIDS research!

I'm glad Hollywood cares about people with AIDS. One need not be a liberal activist to become involved. My wife and I recently contacted our county health officials, and they agreed to introduce us to a local resident suffering from AIDS so that we could share friendship and support. But we should also help people dying of cancer, heart disease, cystic fibrosis, muscular dystrophy, Marfan syndrome, and other illnesses. Just because cancer patients don't storm St. Patrick's Cathedral and interrupt worship services doesn't mean their disease deserves less medical research than does the HIV virus.

Whenever some radical religious group behaves like the militant gay lobby, the secular media pillories it. But the AIDS lobby seems to be able to do anything it pleases, no matter how outrageous or downright nasty, and nobody in the general media establishment dares hold it accountable. Gays can make illogical or slanderous statements, and few politicians will challenge their veracity. Why? Because people with AIDS have the first politically protected disease in American history.

I'm wondering: Why don't liberal activists wear little red ribbons for people with high blood pressure? Why doesn't Hollywood sponsor more fund-raising galas for non-HIV diseases? At the 1992 Democratic National Convention, people with AIDS and homosexuals were celebrated to the point that I wondered whether many delegates had any regard for the traditional family unit ordained by God.

I'm not suggesting that Republicans are more righteous or moral than Democrats. The GOP also has serious problems. While the Democratic party marches to the militant tune of special-interest groups, the Republican party is manipulated by big business. Many vote conservatively simply because they have wealth worth conserving. They don't want it taxed away or robbed, and that explains why they support fiscal restraint and law enforcement. Despite their promotion of God and country, some conservatives show little interest in genuine spirituality.

Where is the social conscience of the conservatives? Beyond mere tokenism and sloganeering, do we see much concern for racial and gender injustice, poverty, and the environment?

I do appreciate that Republicans at least speak up for family values and personal morality. Former Vice President Quayle suffered persecution for his "Murphy Brown" remarks, but did you read the full text of his speech? In my opinion, any reasonable Christian would concur with his statements on marriage and the family. It's easy to understand why the entertainment industry finds family values such a threat, since Hollywood makes so many billions with its sin business. We may legitimately question the motives of some conservatives with their rhetoric, but I salute them for defending moral standards.

I also believe Republicans are generally correct that the government should cut spending rather than raising taxes—if only they would also cut the perks for the wealthy! But they won't do that. Many conservatives just don't seem to care if the rich get richer and the poor get poorer. And I'm afraid some of them would rather close down abortion clinics than open up their hearts to women in crisis.

Another problem with Republicans is their party's national platform, which poses a severe threat to the preservation of religious liberty. If the world lasts until 1996, may the Lord have mercy should Republican right-wing extremists take charge of the presidential campaign. We could expect a scenario that fulfills Revelation 13.

I suspect some conservatives would be surprised to discover that the Lord isn't a registered Republican. From my reading of the New Testament, Jesus didn't ride an elephant into Jerusalem! Of course, our Lord isn't a Democrat either. He doesn't take sides in partisan politics—and I don't think Adventists should either. Not as a church and not as individuals. We should, however, be knowledgeable of what's happening around us. We should also get involved in the big moral issues of our time. Let's not be so engrossed in discussions about soybeans and wedding rings that we forget about equal rights for women, environmental stewardship, and helping the homeless.

To that end, I dedicate this book. You might call it a hot potatoes dinner that sets a plate for someone outside the Adventist cocoon. These are the subjects that get airtime on the six o'clock news, the things your neighbors are arguing and worrying about. For you to reach them, it will help to offer an Adventist biblical perspective on the great moral issues of our time.

I hope you find that in this book. If you don't agree with me, the Lord will forgive you!

Don't mind my touch of humor now and then. Even though these are serious subjects, we ought to enjoy exploring them! And, of course, what you read in these pages reflects my personal convictions. I am not speaking for the General Conference, its Ministerial Association, or *Ministry* magazine. And, please accept what I'm saying as a conversation starter rather than a lecture.

My main concern as we wrestle with reality is maintaining a Christ-centered balance. You've seen pictures of Japanese sumo wrestlers. If they lose their balance, they are out of the contest. So with us as we wrestle with reality in these pages. If we lose our balance, we've lost everything.

Keep that in mind as you turn the page so we can discuss whether it's a sin to own a gun.

Chapter 1

Bearing Arms

(Handguns and noncombatancy)

Your red digital alarm clock reads 2:18. The bedroom is dark and quiet. Suddenly you hear something, a muffled noise downstairs. Must be the silly cat knocking the family Bible off the coffee table.

No, it's something bigger. You lift your head from the pillow.

Floorboards are squeaking. Something—someone—is prowling around the living room!

Footsteps approach the bottom of the stairway. Chills race along your spine, and you clutch your blanket in terror. Then the flickering beam of a flashlight moves up the stairs. Your heart is pounding at your throat as a hulking form emerges from the shadows. Through the open bedroom doorway you see him in the hallway, shining his light slowly this way and that.

Now he sees you. It's too late for 911. He's coming toward you! What does he want! Robbery? Rape? Worse? Entering into your room, the masked man stands there, gun in hand. Then he advances toward your bed. You scream.

And then you wake up, shaking and sobbing in cold sweat. It's nothing, just a nightmare. You're OK. But for thousands of crime victims every night, there's no waking out of such a nightmare.

Let's wrestle with the reality of what should be done about the crime wave that floods our nation with innocent blood. Is it wrong to buy a gun for self-protection? Is it wrong for a Christian to bear

13

arms as a police officer protecting the community? On a national level, is it wrong to raise an army to protect against invasion?

Important questions of global importance. Let's begin in your own neighborhood. How come criminals are free to stalk our streets? Even in our own homes they hold us hostage to fear. Do we need to call out the National Guard to recapture our cities and towns?

A time for terror

Whatever happened to the good old days when people could walk city streets at night, unafraid and unmolested? Our police are brave and capable. Yes, we need more of them, but basically the problem doesn't lie with law enforcement. The average citizen isn't the problem, either. Even now, in the nineties, most people are decent, hard-working, and law-abiding. But some are not, and it takes only a few criminals to terrorize an entire region. Even one can do it alone.

I'm thinking of Richard Ramirez, a devil-worshiping drifter known as the Night Stalker. Ramirez terrorized southern California in the mid 1980s, slipping into homes to kill men and rape their wives. Every night when the sun went down, millions slipped into the shadows of fear. Whenever I left the house, my terrified children tried to pull me back and make me stay. They didn't want the Night Stalker to kill them too.

I'd like to suggest that it's high time we turned the tables on criminals and terrorize *them*! Some would say that's not being nice, talking about terrorizing criminals. So much for human opinion. Let's see what the Lord says:

> Rulers are not a terror to good works, but to evil. Do you want to be unafraid of the authority? Do what is good, and you will have praise from the same. For he is God's minister to you for good. But if you do evil, be afraid; for he does not bear the sword in vain; for he is God's minister, an avenger to execute wrath on him who practices evil (Romans 13:3, 4).

What do you think of that? The Bible—the New Testament, in fact—says that law enforcement officers with their weapons are ministers of God, maintaining law and order, protecting life and property.

We Adventists believe in law, don't we? So why aren't there more Adventist law-enforcement officers?

A woman I used to work with kept a picture of her son by her desk. I asked her what he did for a living. She seemed ashamed to tell me he had chosen a career in law enforcement. Sabbath School teachers had told her it was wrong to be a policeman because police officers carry guns. I told her that, according to the Bible, she could be proud of her son as one of God's ministers. He was a minister of mercy to protect the helpless and a minister of wrath to those who prey upon them. You should have seen the relief and joy on her face when she saw in the Bible that her son was in "the ministry."

In our next chapter we'll come back to Romans 13 to consider the meaning of wrath and also whether God believes the death penalty is just.

Lawyers and law enforcement

Working closely with police officers to bring offenders to justice are prosecuting attorneys. Opposing them vigorously are defense attorneys, too many of whom manipulate and exploit the legal system, caring everything about liberty for their clients but little about justice for all society.

Some defense lawyers seem determined to undermine society's efforts to come to terms with crime. On a national level they often work through the American Civil Liberties Union (ACLU). One of the most powerful advocacy groups in the United States, the ACLU must be commended for its efforts to protect the underdog, particularly in the area of religious liberty. Unfortunately, in my opinion, the ACLU goes to extremes in promoting individual freedoms at the expense of society as a whole. Why can't there be an organization called the American Civil Justice Union? Shouldn't attorneys be equally concerned with justice?

I'm not running down the law profession, please understand.

My son Steve may become a lawyer, with my fervent encouragement. I've told him he could have a tremendous ministry in any one of the many specialties of law practice. Prosecuting attorneys are an indispensable element of law enforcement in administering justice. Defense attorneys also serve a vital role, protecting the accused against a false conviction and, when the client is guilty, making sure that all mitigating factors are considered. Many dedicated public defenders work for a comparative pittance, considering their skills and education.

So much for criminal law. In civil cases a good lawyer can protect you from frivolous lawsuits in our greedy society. If the Internal Revenue Service accuses you of tax evasion, a competent attorney can save you from undeserved hardship and even bankruptcy. In everything from buying a house to starting a business to filing a patent, responsible attorneys can be a tremendous blessing to the individual. They serve the national good as well. Were it not for the volunteer efforts of civil rights lawyers, this country would have made but little progress toward racial equality.

Unlawful lawyers

So I thank God for lawyers, and I wish that was all that needed to be said about them. But we must consider the other side of the coin. Some lawyers, in performing a valuable service for their clients, damage society in the process. I'm thinking of the infamous ambulance chasers, who help accident victims (and themselves) get overgenerous settlements while causing insurance premiums and health-care costs to skyrocket.

Many lawyers don't appear to view their profession as anything resembling a community service. And in their private moments, some of them don't deny it. I've sat next to lawyers on airplanes while they've entertained me with joke after joke about the dirty tricks of their profession. Lawyers of integrity—and there are still many of them—feel outraged about the antics of unscrupulous peers.

Basically, my gripe with the legal profession as commonly practiced is twofold: (1) that too many lawyers take financial advantage of people, especially those in crisis, and (2) that many lawyers don't hesitate to use deception to win their case, even if it means cheating the innocent of justice. Let me elaborate.

Too many lawyers care more about winning a favorable verdict than they do about right and wrong in their fierce determination to win favorable verdicts. Even when their motivation is compassion rather than greed, this blind bias on behalf of their clients harms society.

Consider a rape trial. Some defense attorneys, even if they know their client committed a crime, will often point the finger of blame at the victim herself. They may accuse her of lying and needlessly pry into her personal life. Seeking to get their client acquitted, they impute to the innocent victim awful motives that they know aren't true. No deception is too dark or dirty for some defense lawyers in ruining the reputation of the victim and denying her justice. This is an outrage. I believe such lawyers themselves become rapists of a kind, using the legal system to strip away the rights of the victim, invade her privacy, and leave her more embarrassed and devastated than she was after the original crime.

"Wait a minute," some would protest. "It's a lawyer's job to defend the client, doing whatever it takes to get an acquittal." No, not at the cost of withholding the truth. Consider me idealistic if you wish, but I don't think anyone has a right to fabricate a legal case based upon known falsehood.

A few years ago a drunken driver going east on the westbound lanes of the Ventura Freeway nearly killed me and my two children. Instead, he murdered a family of four in a car behind me. The Los Angeles county prosecutor flew me twice across the country to testify at the second-degree murder trial. The defense attorney tried to twist the facts in his client's favor and make me a liar. Had not his efforts been so obviously deceptive, he might have cast doubt upon my honesty and integrity.

I don't think he had a right to do that to me—and I was just a witness. What about denying justice to the family of the victims?

Legal abomination

Telling lies is not permissible for the prosecution, so why should it be OK for the defense to distort the truth? If a guilty man is turned loose, the victim is not only discredited but subjected to the additional danger of physical vengeance. Beyond that, another man may be charged with the unsolved crime, thus endangering an innocent person.

We don't like it when we hear about prosecutors bending the truth to convict innocent people. Isn't it just as wrong for a defense attorney to fabricate falsehoods to release the guilty? The Bible says: "He who justifies the wicked, and he who condemns the just, both of them alike are an abomination to the Lord" (Proverbs 17:15). Christian attorneys should ponder that text carefully, lest they turn their God-given ministry into an abomination.

The whole legal system operates on the truth, the whole truth, and nothing but the truth; lawyers must not imagine themselves a privileged exception. You expect the accused to lie in court if he is guilty. After all, he's a criminal. But what about his lawyer who joins him in falsehood? Beyond showing disrespect for the court, isn't this aiding and abetting a criminal? Whether the motive is financial or misplaced compassion, it's an obstruction of justice.

Instead of denying the truth, an attorney of integrity will argue the case on mitigating circumstances (which we will discuss in the next chapter). This still leaves plenty of room to operate in defense of the client. Yes, he molested that child, but he himself was molested as a child. That doesn't excuse him, but it mitigates his guilt. If a criminal is not willing to confess and tell the truth, let him find himself a lawyer willing to do business on another basis. He shouldn't have to look too far.

I know my convictions about the legal system sound ridiculously naive and impractical to most veterans of the courtroom jungle, conditioned as they are to dealing in deception. But I invite anyone to show me from the Bible how Christian attorneys can base their law practice on anything less than the truth.

One more point to ponder about attorneys. If they manage to manipulate the justice system and get a criminal released to prowl the streets again, aren't they partially responsible for any additional crimes committed? Haven't they turned their legal practice into a dangerous and potentially deadly weapon?

Handguns in the house

So much for keeping offenders behind bars after they are arrested. Now let's talk about apprehending them and putting them in jail. It might help to have a gun around the house to subdue a criminal, but some Christians think it's a lack of faith to arm themselves. They suggest that we should depend upon God instead of a gun.

Certainly God, through His angels, is our ultimate defense, but consider this: When a burglar breaks into the house and you call the police—do you ask the officers to leave their guns outside? Doesn't the officer whom you summon become an extension of yourself? Doesn't his gun become, in effect, your gun? I think so, and I don't think there is anything wrong with that. Remember, it's really God's gun that he's carrying as your defender.

I'm not suggesting that we all run out and buy guns. Perhaps a better idea would be to have in one's pocket, purse, or night stand a little cannister of a nonlethal spray deterrent. It isn't a good idea to have guns with children around the house, unless the guns are really secured. There's also the danger of mistakenly shooting a family member in the dark. Such things happen too often. Careful training is essential before purchasing a gun, and the required seven-day waiting period for buying a handgun is one way to limit impulsive use of firearms. Gun ownership should be carefully restricted to responsible citizens, keeping as many weapons as possible out of the hands of criminals.

But having mentioned those provisions, what sin is there in having a weapon to protect your family? I know an Adventist minister who keeps a gun; he told me he almost had to use it recently to shoot an intruder. Self-defense, you understand. Do you think that would have been a sin?

Well, if faith involves leaving oneself vulnerable to crime, why waste money on burglar alarms and night watchmen? Why buy locks for doors? Don't lock your car, either; leave the key inside and trust the Lord! If somebody wants to take it, let him have it. You can always ride your bike to church. Material things aren't that important, anyway, so really trust the Lord and cancel your insurance!

You know I don't mean all that. Keep your insurance. While we trust the Lord to protect us, there are prudent measures we must take on our own behalf. Self-protection of various kinds is legitimate and necessary in a world of sin. However, there is one difference between a police officer's weapon and one I might own. Being a minister of the gospel and not God's minister of wrath, I'm not authorized to enforce justice. My responsibility as a private citizen is to turn the criminal over to law enforcement officials.

War and noncombatancy

Now let's think about bearing arms on a larger level. Does a nation have the right to defend itself with force against aggressors? Why not?

Actually, there is a difference between military action and a citizen defending himself against crime. In warfare a soldier is not shooting a criminal but another citizen in the service of his country, perhaps drafted against his will. Killing him would be taking innocent life. One might persuasively argue that anyone who participates, however unwillingly, in an armed effort promoting tyranny becomes an agent of aggression. This may be true, but it's still a tragedy when teenagers are taken from their families, turned into soldiers, and killed on the battlefield while attacking another country. Nevertheless, I believe a nation has the right to defend its territory against invasion, no matter the cost.

Is it ever appropriate for a country to wage offensive warfare, rather than just defending against a foreign invasion? What about the United States' "invasion" of Somalia in which the army used its overwhelming weaponry to open floodgates of relief to starving children? Would it have troubled your conscience to have brandished a rifle and chased away the wicked warlords of famine? How about a military hostage-rescue mission? Although most wars are fought to gain wealth and land—and that is immoral—other wars overthrow tyranny. Tell me, would it have been a sin to get in an army tank and blast through the gates of Hitler's concentration camps to liberate starving prisoners? One of my best friends spent many years in a Communist dungeon, suffering for his faith. He and his fellow Christian prisoners wished that the American army would invade the country and restore them to their families while establishing religious freedom. Surely wars of greed and conquest are wrong, but there is such a thing as a just war. We must not condemn those who fight in it.

Did you know that during the persecutions of the Middle Ages, Protestants sometimes organized armies to defend themselves against invading forces? Read about it in *The Great Controversy*; notice, for example, pages 116-118. God gave them miraculous victories over the persecuting armies.

But what of the poor soldiers killed by those defending their own wives and children? Death is a tragedy, but there comes a point where a cause is so unjust that anyone who fights for it— even under duress when drafted—can expect the Lord to turn the tide of battle against him.

Of course, the church as an institution has no business raising armies for any reason at all; I believe churches should avoid entanglement in politics altogether. But Christians as individuals can vote and run for office—and also fight for freedom.

Adventist missionaries in World War II rejoiced when the Allies liberated Singapore and the work of God could continue throughout the Pacific theater. Was that wrong? Were we supposed to be neutral? Let's be honest. We rejoice when the armies of freedom prevail, and there's no reason to be ashamed of it. True Christians everywhere lament the death of innocent people, even national enemies. Blind patriotism is wrong, but we need not shed tears of shame when our nation faithfully fights for liberty and justice. War is hell, as the saying goes, but there are times when tyranny and oppression are so great that armed intervention is a service to world peace.

Patriotic noncombatancy

Having said all that, I fully support the traditional position of the Seventh-day Adventist Church regarding noncombatancy. We avoid the absolute pacifist extreme that shuns any involvement with the military; instead, we encourage our young people to serve as medics—but not as armed soldiers. It's neither unchristian nor unpatriotic to be a medic; indeed, one serves the country just as much in that role as with a rifle. The ministry of healing is always needed, and noncombatancy as a medic is the safest way to walk the tightrope between rendering service to

Caesar and serving God.

While the church is correct in recommending noncombatancy, I believe it should allow individuals to decide for themselves what position to take on this issue. In many places in the world, requiring church members to be noncombatants would bring an unnecessary jail sentence. Even in North America and other countries where it's possible to avoid bearing arms, the church is not a cult demanding that everybody must do exactly the same thing. While we should hold to certain fundamental truths that define us as a denomination, God has created each of us with his or her own conscience. "Let each be fully convinced in his own mind" (Romans 14:5).

Some Adventist medics carry sidearms in case the enemy would try to interrupt their missions of mercy. Their handguns are totally defensive rather than offensive. Nevertheless, for conscience' sake, others carry no weapon whatever. Again, let each one be fully persuaded in his or her own mind.

Whether or not to carry any kind of weapon on a battlefield is a matter for continuing discussion. But there's one battleground where Americans definitely should fight and win—our neighborhoods, towns, and cities. Whatever it takes, let's get criminals off the streets and behind bars. We owe it to our children.

Is the death penalty an appropriate and effective deterrent against murder? I've come to some strong convictions about that. Turn the page, and I'll explain why.

Chapter 2

The Death Penalty

(Criminal justice)

My wife and I were driving home from the mall this afternoon, having completed our traditional Sunday window shopping, when we passed a wreath of flowers by the roadside. It marked the spot where a few days ago a young mother was killed while taking her daughter to her first day of school. It was a particularly horrible crime.

A man and a teenager had approached Pamela Basu as she waited at a stop sign for traffic to clear. They forced her outside the car. Then, as the frantic mother tried to reach back inside to rescue her daughter, they drove away with tires screeching. Pamela's arm became entangled in the seat belt, and she was dragged along like a rag doll. The criminals scraped the car against a barbed-wire fence until the dead mother dropped onto the roadside. Then they stopped the car, tossed the little girl on the side of the road, and took off.

Howard County police finally caught up with the murderers, whose family members have already begun making excuses for them. Everybody I know is furious.

Is it wrong to have a passion for justice? Should society punish criminals or just rehabilitate them? And what about the death penalty for murderers?

The subject of civil justice stirs up strong emotions and sparks conflict among equally earnest Christians. Let's try to set aside our preconceptions and recall what the Bible says:

> Rulers are not a terror to good works, but to evil. Do you
> want to be unafraid of the authority? Do what is good, and
> you will have praise from the same. For he is God's minis-
> ter to you for good. But if you do evil, be afraid; for he does
> not bear the sword in vain; for he is God's minister, an
> avenger to execute wrath on him who practices evil (Romans
> 13:3, 4).

God's loving wrath

Some Christians see wrath as a passive attribute of God where-
by He simply lets sinners reap what they have sown. It's true, in
one sense, that sinners destroy themselves, but God doesn't just
stand by and let it happen. He stands up for the oppressed against
those who do them harm.

Consider the example of Jesus. The New Testament reveals
our Saviour's passion for the victims of society and His fervent
sense of justice. He was outraged when greedy money-changers
took advantage of poor worshipers and turned His Father's house
into a den of thieves. He became "indignant" when His disciples
forbade children from coming to Him (see Mark 10:14, NIV).
Evidently the Good Shepherd noticed the disappointed faces of
His lambs, and He became angry at those who stopped them from
climbing onto His lap.

Surprising as it may seem, it was really Christ's love that
made Him angry. He cared enough about the children to become
indignant at the threat of losing His friendship with them.
Human parents also become outraged—because of their love—
when their children are mistreated or molested. Likewise a loving
wife is incensed when her husband shares his body with another
woman. If she didn't get upset, we would question her own
commitment to the relationship, wouldn't we?

Nevertheless, many Christians feel they must minimize or
even deny the reality of divine wrath in the heart of a loving
God. Shouldn't we be thankful for a Lord who cares enough to
get angry? How could we respect a God who had no passion for
justice, who could witness all the world's murder, racism, oppres-

sion, and immorality without being stirred up, deeply moved with outrage?

God is concerned about the lesser things too. He is angry when an auto mechanic cheats a single mother out of money needed for groceries. He is incensed when a drunken hit-and-run driver slaughters a child on her bicycle. He is enraged when persecuting powers shed the blood of His people. And yes, He is indignant when modern Pharisees gossip over the struggles of baby believers.

Even so, there is a vast difference between the holy wrath of God and the "righteous" indignation you and I feel. Though the Lord gets angry about sin, He maintains His love for sinners. You and I sometimes have a problem doing that, don't we? Our Father in heaven sees what we don't see; His heart is bigger than ours.

God hates sin but loves sinners

God abhors child abuse, but He knows that most molesters were themselves abused as children. He hates the crime of vehicular manslaughter, but He understands that the driver who got drunk had only been trying to escape his own emotional pain. God despises gossip, but He also pities the hypocrite whose lack of spiritual security leads him to flaunt his own counterfeit righteousness.

God hates murder, but He understands the circumstances that can lead to such a terrible crime. One of the two arrested for carjacking and the murder of Pamela Basu was a sixteen-year-old boy who had evidently been a somewhat reluctant accomplice. His major mistake was to befriend and accompany the older man, a convicted felon who had just been released on bond from jail.

Mitigating circumstances

There was no reason for the teenager to become an accomplice to murder. He should have tried to save the life of the mother or at least jump out of the car and run away to tell police. Nevertheless, the circumstances of the case mitigate his guilt.

Crime is always inexcusable; otherwise, it shouldn't be considered crime. But sometimes people get desperate, and they do something rash—such as rob a bank. A mother might steal food for her baby. She shouldn't have done it, but at least the degree of her guilt is lessened by the motivation for her crime. Poverty is a mitigating factor in committing crime. So is an abusive environment, either in the home or in the neighborhood. Remember, though, there is still no justification for evildoing. If a person suffered a terrible childhood, here's what we should tell him or her: "We're sorry about your circumstances. Let us help you recover with counseling, education, and opportunities for a better life. Above all, come to know the healing love of God. But if you decide to turn on society, the oppressed becoming the oppressor, then you are making victims of your own. The helping hand of mercy will become the steel fist of justice."

Insanity is a unique mitigating circumstance. In such cases the one who committed the crime either didn't have the capacity to know what he or she was doing, or was unable to control himself. There are comparatively few such situations; nevertheless, criminal lawyers who cannot deny the involvement of their client will often argue insanity as a last-ditch defense.

John Hinkley, Jr., who nearly robbed the free world of its leader by shooting President Reagan, got off the hook by pleading not guilty by reason of insanity. Did he really not know what he was doing? Could he not have stopped himself?

Hinkley's lawyers managed to convince the jury he was insane. And so the attempted murderer went through a few months of enforced hospitalization before he announced that he was healed. As if to say, "Thank you very much for the counseling and the rap sessions. I'm better now. So clear the way, and I'm out of here."

Not so fast, young man. America doesn't want you prowling the streets again and risking the life of our current president. Besides, some of us are not convinced that you were innocent in the first place. And if you weren't genuinely insane, then what you did was inexcusable.

Pity mixed with anger

God, in His holiness, can never excuse sin of any kind, but in His mercy He regards the circumstances of sinners. He understands the confused emotions, the frustration, and the low self-esteem that contribute to evil behavior. And so His anger against sin is mingled with pity for sinners.

We see this when Jesus healed the man with a withered hand. The coldhearted religious authorities grumbled about that miracle of mercy, you recall. Christ "looked around at them with *anger, being grieved* by the hardness of their hearts" (Mark 3:5, emphasis supplied). The word translated "anger" expresses an extremely strong emotion, usually translated as "wrath." Along with such rage, however, Christ was "grieved." He actually felt sorry for the heartless legalists who were condemning Him. He knew the circumstances of their environment that helped shape their intolerant attitude.

Grief and wrath—they go together in the loving heart of God. He feels sad when people find escape in sin, and He is also angry about the misery they inflict upon themselves and their victims.

Consider the pain we bring upon each other by breaking God's commandments. Adultery shatters the family circle, crushing the hearts of both spouse and children. Pride turns business associates into mere steppingstones for career advancement. Greed robs the poor. Gluttony blunts one's ability to serve others with the body temple entrusted to us.

Because sin causes such suffering, God hates it and must take action against those who trample upon His commandments. That law defines love, so God must defend its principles in order to preserve His government of love. For the good of the universe, commandment breakers must receive divine wrath. That's why He declares, "Vengeance is Mine, I will repay" (Romans 12:19).

In punishing sinners God is but granting them the reward of their chosen lifestyle. They have sown seeds of selfishness and strife and must therefore reap disaster, "receiving in themselves the penalty of their error which was due" (Romans 1:27). Indeed, there will come a day when "the wrath of God is revealed from heaven against all ungodliness and unrighteousness of men" (Romans 1:18). But remember, the Lord will not unleash His wrath because He has lost His temper. He will be upholding His law of love, fulfilling His responsibilities as the moral Governor of the universe.

Even secular business managers have to enforce rules of operation; chaos results when laws are disregarded. For the benefit of all employees, rebellion against company policy requires punishment.

Suppose you were manager of the local K Mart. A sales associate keeps shoplifting clothes for her baby. You sympathize with her situation as a single parent and, because of her mitigating circumstances, you want to let her off the hook. But how can you manage to do that without making allowances for others who might argue their own situations as excuses to steal? How do you forgive the lawbreaker without opening the floodgates of lawlessness?

Mercy versus justice

Such is the conflict between mercy and justice that the intrusion of sin brought to the heart of God. Love in justice requires punishment of sin, but love in mercy pleads for sinners. The Lord solved this dilemma on the cross by providing in His mercy what His justice requires. The atoning death of Christ makes it possible for God to function as our forgiving Father as well as the moral Governor of His creation. Now He can receive sinners without being soft on sin.

Let's make no mistake about it. God has a passion for justice. He cares about the oppression in the world, the murder, abuse, greed, and warfare. He reacts against evil; if He refused to act in judgment against it, He would not be a holy God. There is nothing unnatural about a righteous God's wrath against evil. Yes, there *is* vengeance; God will repay.

Some Christians suggest that because all of us are sinners, all of us are worthy of wrath. In the spiritual realm, yes, all of us are absolutely unworthy. But in civil society, there is a difference between law-abiding people and those who terrorize them. Suppose the police answered your frantic request to arrest a burglar—but they arrested you instead! They invited the criminal to sleep in your bed while they handcuffed you and hauled you off to jail! Well, why not, if both of you are equally guilty? What difference would it make which one they arrested?

Obviously, we must distinguish between civil guilt and spiritual guilt, rendering unto Caesar versus rendering unto God. It sounds very spiritual to say that society should pardon criminals just as God pardons sinners. But imagine the chaos such a policy would cause. Immediately upon their profession of repentance, we would have to unlock jail cells and set the prisoners free. On top of that, we would need to apologize to murderers and rapists for failing to represent God's unconditional love to them by confining them. We would need to throw open the prison doors and say, "We don't condemn you! Now go, and please try to sin no more. But if you do attack someone and the police arrest you, don't worry, we'll let you right back out. Just remember that God loves you, and so do we!"

How would that work?

Or how about this: In His Sermon on the Mount, Jesus instructed us to pray: "Forgive us our debts, as we forgive our debtors" (Matthew 6:12). Imagine calling the toll-free Visa number to announce: "Just as God has forgiven me my spiritual debts, I expect you to forgive my credit card debt." Then call up the bank and have them forgive the car payment. And why not the mortgage too? Jubilee!

Ridiculous, of course, but I think you see the point. There *is* a difference between the civil and religious realm. Understanding this, we can make sense out of Christ's Sermon on the Mount:

> You have heard that it was said, "An eye for an eye and a tooth for a tooth." But I tell you not to resist an evil person. But whoever slaps you on your right cheek, turn the other to him also. If anyone wants to sue you and take away your tunic, let him have your cloak also. And whoever compels you to go one mile, go with him two. Give to him who asks you, and from him who wants to borrow from you do not turn away. You have heard that it was said, "You shall love your neighbor and hate your enemy." But I say to you, love your enemies, bless those who curse you, do good to those who hate you, and pray for those who spitefully use you and persecute you (Matthew 5:38-44).

Radical instruction from our Lord, indeed. What did He mean?

Is it possible He was advocating ideals of interpersonal relationships rather than undermining society's system of justice?

Beware being too literal

To begin with, we must realize that Jesus sometimes used superlative language as a teaching tool, not expecting us to interpret everything literally. Consider His promise: "Whatever things you ask when you pray, believe that you receive them, and you will have them" (Mark 11:24). Superficially this seems like a blank check from heaven, but be careful. You can't pray for a gold Mercedes, and wow, "There it is!" So what did Jesus mean by promising, "*Whatever* you ask, you'll receive?" He meant anything within the circle of God's will, which He will dispense in His own time and way as He deems best for us. Obviously, whether we like it or not, we had better interpret Christ's sayings carefully, or we are setting ourselves up for a big letdown.

Sometimes our Lord used exaggeration as a teaching tool—such as the time He taught that it's easier for a camel to pass through the eye of a needle than for a rich person to be saved. His vivid imagery stretched the truth, no doubt, yet in doing so Christ fixed it forever in our memory. However, He never intended for us to take His simple statements and read too much into them. Now we can ask the question: What did Jesus mean about turning the other cheek? Are we supposed to let people push us and our loved ones around without kindly, firmly telling them that we are children of God and expect to be treated as such? Does the Lord want the victim of an assault to tell her attacker: "What you just did was very sinful, but if you ever want to do it again, the Lord requires me to submit to you"? No, the Lord wasn't making His people the playthings of criminals.

What about "an eye for an eye"? If you noticed the context of that statement, Jesus was referring to interpersonal relationships. We shouldn't go out and take our own revenge—that's the role of law enforcement as God's appointed agent of vengeance to equalize injustice.

In the courtroom, "an eye for an eye" is the only policy that's fair for both victim and criminal. If a man knocked out his neighbor's eye, the neighbor couldn't ask for him to be blinded in both eyes. And if he knocked out one tooth, the penalty was the equivalent loss of one tooth—not five. The penalty had to harmonize with the damage suffered. This was only fair, and it also stemmed the tide of crime.

The Lord never intended for innocent citizens to walk the streets in fear. Violent criminals belong in jail for a long time. Yes, they are still human beings, and we should seek to rehabilitate and educate them to someday become productive citizens. Meanwhile, let's keep them off the streets until they have paid the penalty for their crimes and are no longer a threat. Since prisons are already overcrowded, we must build more of them. It's expensive to care for prisoners and keep them confined, but far less costly than having them loose on the street committing more crimes.

Charles Colson of Watergate fame, who for years has conducted a ministry to prisoners, suggests that jail cells be reserved for those who pose a physical threat to society. For nonviolent offenders, he says, restitution rather than incarceration is the answer. White collar criminals who are no physical threat should be fined heavily and then allowed to keep working so they can pay back those they defrauded.

I would add that for those convicted of driving drunk, we should confiscate their vehicles and use the sales to fund their treatment. For nonviolent drug dealers, repossess the proceeds of their crime (as the government has begun doing) and invest them in the war against drugs and in treatment for drug users. For the addicts themselves, unless they are dangerous, require them to get treatment and also make them do community service, such as picking up garbage and painting over graffiti.

Those who hurt people financially should be penalized financially. Those who harm people physically should be physically incarcerated. And what about those who commit murder? Should they also receive the equivalent of their crime?

Capital punishment

Never, you may say. The Bible says, "Thou shalt not kill" (Exodus 20:13, KJV).

Actually the word *kill* is better translated "murder," as many modern versions translate this verse. Capital punishment is not forbidden in the Bible. In fact, both Old and New Testaments specifically endorse the death penalty. God leaves no doubt about the propriety of capital punishment: "Whoever sheds man's blood, by man his blood shall be shed" (Genesis 9:6). So the Lord Himself established the ultimate punishment—and He did it long before the Mosaic era with its ceremonial laws of the old covenant.

We have already discussed the biblical concept of enforcing an equivalent penalty as the only way to maintain justice: "You shall give life for life, eye for eye, tooth for tooth, hand for hand, foot for foot, burn for burn, wound for wound, stripe for stripe" (Exodus 21:23-25). For murder, according to these verses, the only just penalty is life for life.

You might want to remind me here that since only God can give life, only He should take it. Isn't that exactly what He is doing through His minister of civil vengeance, the law enforcement officer? Remember how the Bible describes government authorities: "If you do evil, be afraid; for he does not bear the sword in vain; for he is God's minister, an avenger to execute wrath on him who practices evil" (Roman 13:4). The sword here is an instrument of death. Not a simple little knife, as some opponents of capital punishment suggest, but the same weapon through which the disciple James received capital punishment by order of Herod (see Acts 12:1, 2).

God takes action against evil. His wrath against evildoers is not a passive attribute; He doesn't simply let sinners run their course. If He did, how could He be a God of justice?

Not a deterrent?

Many of my merciful and compassionate friends strenuously object to capital punishment. They have some legitimate concerns. Let's consider these.

They say, first of all, that the death penalty isn't a deterrent against murder. That's difficult to prove or disprove, since few murderers are ever executed. Even after being sentenced to death, convicts and their lawyers endlessly manipulate the legal system. Not until the death penalty is enforced regularly and consistently can we truly measure the deterrent factor.

One thing is certain: the death penalty eliminates repeat offenses. As long as a criminal is alive, he can escape and do further harm. That's what happened with Willie Horton, you recall. And in Virginia not long ago, six convicted murderers broke out of prison and terrorized the community. That would never have happened had their death sentences been executed.

Actually the whole discussion about deterrence misses the point of the death sentence. It's a penalty, a punishment. "Life for life," the Bible decrees. Those who murder human life have forfeited their own right to life. That's God's way, and it's only fair.

You may be wondering how I can promote the death penalty while (as you will discover) being pro-life regarding abortion. There's no inconsistency whatever when you remember that capital punishment preserves innocent life by removing those who destroy it. The reason a father of a toddler might kill a six-foot rattlesnake in the backyard is to preserve life by removing its threat. Murderers by definition are merchants of death. They must lose their lives in order for additional victims to save theirs.

But there can be no reversal after the death penalty! my friends argue. True, so guilt must be proven beyond question. What about the potential for a mistaken death sentence? That's the reason for the appeals process. I concede that a risk remains that some innocent person may still die. Innocent people die in automobile accidents too, but on balance the risks are acceptable in view of overall benefits to society. So it is, I believe, with the death penalty.

We must acknowledge that capital punishment has not always been applied fairly, particularly with minorities. This is a terrible problem, and our legal system must take firm steps to rectify it. But this argument is not really with the death penalty itself, but with how it is applied.

What about God's grace toward sinners? While the life of Jesus modeled God's grace, His death proved that God also up-holds justice. If God didn't believe in the death penalty, Jesus wouldn't have needed to die for our salvation.

I confess that I struggle over the execution of the death

penalty. I've preached in prisons and visited condemned murderers. Many read my books and write to me. They have become my friends and brothers. However, I cannot escape the sad truth that they have made a fatal mistake and must suffer the consequences of civil justice. Their lives must be rendered unto Caesar—but their souls can still be saved unto God. Even though they must die for their crimes, they can have eternal life in Jesus. Indeed, many death-row criminals have confessed their sins, accepted Christ, and died in faith. I'm looking forward to meeting them in heaven.

Yearning for justice

Along with my acquaintance with murderers, I've also befriended the families of murder victims. I've noticed that they have a fundamental yearning that justice will be done and the killers be put to death. Yes, they know their loved ones are dead and nothing will bring them back this side of the resurrection— we need not remind them of that. But they believe there is something obscene about a murderer continuing to live while his victim is silent in the grave. Even though they may desire that the murderer is saved for heaven, they still want justice served down here.

And I don't blame them. Let's stop making them feel guilty. What a terrible thing to do to those who have already suffered more than we can imagine! Too often well-meaning moralists lecture the families of murder victims about the need to forgive and forget. I think of friends who came home one night to discover their children murdered. They were standing in their driveway in shock, red and yellow lights flashing from ambulances waiting to carry away the sheet-shrouded bodies. Suddenly a minister drove up, walked over, put his arms around their shoulders, and admonished them about their responsibility to forgive the murderer.

Can you imagine! Forgiveness is one thing, but we must never forget that justice must be served. God says so. If you disagree, please show me in the Bible that civil punishment is inappropriate in our crime-ridden society. Let's not take the divine gift of justice from the loved ones of murder victims; it's an important, though inadequate, consolation for them.

Many of those families have nightmares that the murderer will break out of jail and kill them too. Witnesses who have testified at the trials also live in fear of their lives. Often the murderer explicitly vows revenge, and as long as he is alive, he might escape. More likely, some well-meaning but weak-minded parole board decides that the murderer has served enough time and turns him loose to prowl the streets again. The only relief from such a possibility is the death of the murderer. Finally everyone can rest in peace and feel safe again.

Criminals need the Lord

While society must protect itself against those who harm life and property, let's remember that all of us are sinners. Even though we may be law-abiding citizens, we would be lost for eternity without the mercy of God. Our hope of heaven is not based on any goodness in ourselves but rather on the grace of God through Christ's sacrifice on the cross. Even as His murderers were nailing Him to the cross, Jesus still loved them. Surely we can go and do likewise.

Chapter 3

Our Unsuspected Sin

(Racism in the church)

Paradise, they said it was. And so it seemed to me that sunny afternoon in Hawaii. Watching the coconut palms swaying gently as the surf rolled in, I stretched on the soft white sand and basked in the friendly sunshine. Everything was relaxing and delightful, until I left the beach and strolled toward a nearby restroom. While approaching the cinder-block building, I passed a gang of hulking native young men who stared at me fiercely.

"Hey, white trash," they taunted, "come back here!" I kept walking, looking straight ahead. They trailed me into the dark restroom and cornered me. *This could be trouble*, I realized as they pelted me with obscenities. One of them snarled, "Why don't you go home?"

"I'd like to do that," I replied, "if you'll get out of my way and let me through." I took a step toward the door.

They wouldn't budge. This was getting scary. I breathed a quick prayer and shouted, "In the name of Jesus Christ, get out of my way!" Immediately they cleared a path to freedom, muttering blasphemies against our Lord as I made my escape.

Once outside, I spotted a police car cruising by and ran toward it. The rowdies, emerging from the restroom, saw where I was heading and took off in the opposite direction. I flagged the officer and hastily explained the situation. The two of us gave chase. The young men ducked into a drainage pipe, scrambled underneath a highway, and disappeared into a sugar cane field.

Although my tormentors managed to avoid arrest, at least I had the satisfaction of turning the tables on them. To some degree, at least, justice had prevailed. Case closed.

What if I were black?

My encounter with the Aloha boys taught me firsthand something of the rottenness of racism. Being an Anglo adult male, I usually go about my business unmolested by it. Such would not necessarily be the case if my skin were a different color. The sad reality is that America is not yet a haven of liberty and justice for all its citizens. Even the church has frequently failed to reveal the love of Christ or basic human decency.

It was a black policeman who came to my rescue in Hawaii. I couldn't help wondering what would have happened if the situation had been reversed. Would a white policeman have been as eager to help a black victim of racism? The unpleasant, inescapable truth is that white law enforcement has often failed its responsibility to African-Americans, a tragic tradition that goes back to the days when KKK mobs lynched their victims unopposed—and sometimes aided—by the sheriff. Justice has been a scarce commodity for black Americans.

It was the failure of justice in the Rodney King case that fueled the fury in Los Angeles. Even officers who witnessed the beating had testified that King was the victim of their peers' excessive force. The most brutal policeman involved had made comments that betrayed rabid racism. Even so, the jury failed to return a single conviction. Who can blame the black community for becoming infuriated?

Confusing one King with another

Let's acknowledge, though, that Rodney King is not the twin of Martin Luther King, Jr. There is a big difference between leading a wild police chase and leading a civil-rights freedom march. Some journalists tried to make a martyr out of someone whose own lawyers dared not place on the witness stand in Simi Valley. King's eloquent appeal to stop the rioting revealed that he had a sensitive side, but a couple of months later his own wife dialed 911 and charged him with threatening her life.

Rodney King was also dangerous and drunk on the fateful night of his arrest. After police finally managed to pull over his speeding white Hyundai, he still refused to cooperate. If he had, as did the other men in his car, he could have saved himself a lot of trouble. Of course, this doesn't exonerate the police for their brutality.

We must assess the rioting in the context of bitter disappointment over the Rodney King verdict. Although justice has never been a friend of the black community, this time things would be different, people thought, given the dramatic and apparently irrefutable documentation of police brutality. Blacks were reassured, "Be patient and let the system do its work." Then, just when justice seemed imminent, the Simi Valley jury returned the verdict that triggered an earthquake registering 10.0 on the disappointment scale. Los Angeles exploded in shock waves of fury at the outrageous injustice.

Unfortunately, many people overreacted, in my opinion, and created an outrage of their own. Blame the Crips and Bloods for exploiting legitimate community anger by sparking the deadly rioting, but remember that thousands of everyday citizens, including Hispanics and whites, accompanied the homicidal "homeboys" as they burned and looted. Shouldn't all participants share some measure of shame and blame for torching their city?

Sister Souljah

After the riot, as the world sifted through the smoking rubble searching for solutions, activist/rap singer Sister Souljah offered her own reaction to what happened: "If black people kill black people every day, why not have a week and kill white people?"

One could hardly imagine a more irresponsible, irrational commentary on how the black community should respond to racial injustice. People of all races gasped in horror at Souljah's rhetoric, yet she managed to appear as an honored guest at a "Rainbow Coalition" convention. After Bill Clinton, at the time a presidential candidate, denounced Souljah's presence, Jesse Jackson spoke up for her. On what basis? "She represents the feelings and hopes of a whole generation of people," Jackson said.

"She should receive an apology" from Clinton.

Did Bill Clinton take political advantage of an opportunity to win the allegiance of white voters? Perhaps so. But the question remains whether Sister Souljah is a legitimate spokesperson for the black community. Most people unacquainted with rap music had never heard of her before. When we look at the person underneath her angry scowl, whom do we find? What influenced her to say what she did?

Souljah's previous name was Lisa Williamson. A few years before, Lisa was a social worker dedicated to helping the needy in New York City, serving in connection with a church group. What she saw, heard, and experienced embittered her against white people—but she also became frustrated with fellow blacks. Specifically, she was alarmed and perplexed that many black youth would rather shoot one another than improve their lot in life. It was from this background that she made her remark that blacks should take a break from destroying one another and take revenge on white people.

How sad that Lisa Williamson, the dedicated young social worker, could lose heart and find hate as Sister Souljah. If she truly "represents the feelings and hopes of a whole generation," then America is bound for big trouble. I would rather believe that Souljah speaks only for a limited number of hard-core, disenchanted disciples. Many black leaders—mayors and members of Congress particularly—joined the majority of African-Americans in lamenting Souljah's inflammatory comments.

Others were strangely quiet. Why? Wouldn't Martin Luther King, Jr., have spoken out against her gospel of violence? I acknowledge a certain amount of disappointment in the muted reaction of some black leaders to the looting and burning, and to the beating of innocent motorists. Again and again on network news programs they said: "We do not condone the violence, but you can understand why young people would act that way."

Well, I'm really trying to understand. Hopeless youth have little incentive to be good to society when society isn't good to them. But does that justify burning down the store where you plan to buy milk the next morning? Arson against one's own community doesn't make sense and deserves outright censure.

I felt especially disappointed with Jesse Jackson's defense of Souljah because in so many ways Jackson deserves our admiration. In the spring of 1991 I attended one of his community rallies in southeast Washington, D.C., and afterward had opportunity for a brief interview with him. I appreciated what he said about black people needing to seize control of their situation by shunning addiction and embracing education. Speaking up for Souljah stands in bleak contrast to that good advice.

On the local level it seems that some community leaders, despite good intentions, waste energy making excuses for problems in the ghetto, such as crime, addiction to welfare, narcotics, and illegitimate sex. No doubt the anger and hopelessness that many African-Americans feel has been born and bred in white racism, but the bitterness and hatred personified in Sister Souljah solves nothing. Instead of looking for ways to blame white people for almost everything, wouldn't it be better to look for ways to stir up the potent moral and spiritual aspirations of the black community?

Fostering racial unity

Such is the situation as I perceive it. Please know that everything you are reading stems from a sense of concern for racial equity. In the past two decades I've tried to do my part to enhance human relations. When I was a student at Columbia Union College, for example, some of us boarded a bus every Sabbath afternoon and went to the ghetto to tutor children. In later years as pastor of a church in southern California, I baptized a black family, ignoring whisperings about "lowering the standards" of the church. The complaints were not only unchristian but irrational as well, since the husband happened to be a distinguished professor at California State University.

Criticism intensified when our pastoral staff added a black minister of music. Then some of the saints observed that many new visitors I invited, people of various races and cultures, failed to reflect the socioeconomic norm of that congregation. Confronting the gossip, I addressed the matter one Sabbath morning. After a sermon on Matthew 25, I invited anyone who could not tolerate what God was doing to attend instead one of the thirteen other Adventist churches in Orange County. As you might expect, that invitation did not go over well, and my ministry to the church spiraled downward.

Looking back, I realize that in taking my stand, I should have mingled tact with courage. Despite my failure, at least the Lord knows I tried to do something about racial prejudice. It's important to me that you also know where my heart is, given the sensitive nature of this subject and the frankness of this evaluation.

Racism is nothing new

The sad fact is that few whites and blacks really understand each other. America suffers other cultural clashes as well, between Anglos and Hispanics; Hispanics and blacks; blacks and Asians; whites and Asians; and everyone, it seems, against the Jews.

Such conflict among contrasting cultures is nothing new. In all times and places, racism has been a problem on this planet. When Jesus walked this earth, the self-righteous religious leaders even segregated the temple courts. On penalty of death, the Jews forbade Gentiles from worshiping with them in the inner sanctums. Archaeologists in 1871 uncovered evidence of this death decree. While digging in the ruins of the temple site in Jerusalem, they found a stone marked with this warning:

No man of another race is to proceed within the partition and enclosing wall about the sanctuary. And one arrested there will have himself to blame for the penalty of death which will be imposed as a consequence.

How very sad. At best, Jews treated the Gentiles with aloofness; at worst, they despised them. And the Gentiles responded in the same spirit, regarding Jews as the scourge of humanity. Literature of Christ's day seethed with this continuous hostility between the races.

Racial conflict has festered through the centuries since New Testament times. The church of the Middle Ages was riddled with antisemitism. During the Spanish Inquisition, for example,

Rome gave Jews the rude choice of either death or a forced conversion to Christianity. The Protestant Reformation celebrated freedom in Christ, but was itself tainted with racism against Jews. Martin Luther's pen, which brought forth so much good, also sprayed antisemitic venom around northern Europe.

Just when the world needed it most, the new American continent opened its arms as a refuge from the Old World's prejudices. Freedom wasn't available to all people, though. We love to talk about the good ship *Mayflower* but would rather not think about the hundreds of slave ships that transported human cargo across the Atlantic.

Bondage in the land of the free

Enshackled Africans who survived the suffocating, nauseating nightmare over the ocean were auctioned into lifelong bondage. Regarded as the property of their masters, slaves had no rights. Men were torn from their families, their wives and daughters often becoming the sexual toys of plantation owners.

So it was that Southern hospitality welcomed the demons of slavery. Even supposedly God-fearing Christians twisted Bible texts to support their hellish practice. Amazing indeed that the enslaved Africans accepted and incorporated Christianity into their culture, as evidenced by the haunting and heart-touching spirituals beloved by music lovers everywhere.

After two centuries of the dark shadow of bondage, a movement to abolish it blossomed between 1830 and 1860. The Second Great Awakening, an intense religious revival in America, fueled abolitionist fervor. Agitation to free the slaves had its base in the North, although a few Southern churches also took a bold stand. Did you know, however, that even most whites who opposed slavery regarded blacks as subhuman—or at best, inferior humans? Most abolitionist societies actually refused membership to blacks! Even "Abraham Lincoln, who opposed the extension of slavery into free territories, stated publicly that he found the idea of Black people being socially equal to White people reprehensible."[1]

It seems incredible that Lincoln, the one who emancipated the slaves and paid for it with his own life, could so seriously misunderstand race relations. Only the grace of God could have orchestrated the freedom of black people, the same sovereign Power that long ago commanded Pharaoh: "Let My people go!"

Even after the American exodus, life for blacks remained bleak here. The best most could manage was to become tenant farmers, "sharecroppers" forever in debt to white landowners. One major positive factor in the later nineteenth century was the movement to provide education for African-Americans. Although the quality of schooling was generally poor, some ex-slaves and their children learned how to attain limited, regional political power. Tragically, whites found ways to strip blacks of their civic progress. "Three types of statutes proved especially effective in preventing Blacks from voting: the poll tax, literacy tests, and the grandfather clause."[2]

The "grandfather clause" specified that citizens were ineligible to vote unless their fathers or grandfathers had voted. This naturally eliminated blacks from entering the voting booth. In 1915 the Supreme Court ruled against this outrage of justice, but discrimination and segregation found other ways to flourish. Meanwhile, blacks found themselves terrorized by white lynch mobs. Many died with a noose encircling their necks.

By the end of World War I, interracial relations had hit bottom. Seeking to escape bondage to their dire circumstances, many blacks during the next several decades moved to northern cities and found menial jobs in factories. Even up north, equality eluded them.

In the 1950s, when Martin Luther King appeared on the American scene, blacks still found themselves forced to the "back of the bus" in many ways. But change was coming. African-American hearts across our land burned with a yearning to finally own the freedoms they had defended in two world wars. Black hands stretched to grasp their fair share of post-war prosperity.

In the 1960s the war for civil rights raged across America. Black Panthers, unwilling any longer to be denied their rights, shouted "Burn, baby, burn!" as Newark, Detroit, and Watts erupted in riots. Martin Luther King, Jr., vigorously opposed their militant tactics, insisting upon weapons of nonviolence—

prayer rallies, freedom rides, and boycotts. Who could forget his ringing proclamation to a cheering crowd at a massive rally for freedom in Washington, D.C.: "Thank God Almighty, I'm free at last!"? Many consider his Wednesday-afternoon speech in 1963 to be a defining moment in the history of the United States.

Murder of a dream

Martin Luther King, Jr., accomplished much of his dream before an assassin's bullet stole him from our generation. Tragically, America's civil rights reformation stalled in the later seventies and took a tailspin in the eighties. Now in the nineties we must rekindle civil rights fervor if we will ever qualify as a "kinder, gentler nation."

Martin Luther King, Jr.'s peaceful revolution reflected the methods of Jesus. Incredibly, though, it was the Hindu leader Gandhi who demonstrated to King how following the example of Christ could influence social change in modern society. If the truth be told (and it must), Christianity in its dealings with African-Americans has failed miserably in reflecting the character of Christ.

Christians in America ought to honor the memory of Martin Luther King, Jr., and the cause for which he died. I've noticed, though, that some of us are not enthusiastic about the holiday that bears King's name. A few years ago when I proposed an article for an Adventist publication about Martin Luther King Day, a blunt rebuff bounced back.

"Why would you want to write about that man?" the editorial assistant chided. "King had character deficiencies."

"Who doesn't?" I argued. "But despite whatever supposed or real faults King had, let's remember what he stood for. By advocating nonviolence, he made America a better place, even for white people.

"Besides," I continued, "the day that bears King's name transcends the man himself. It provides opportunity for all Americans to celebrate cleansing from slavery's dark chapter in our national history. The Martin Luther King holiday also gives us time to search our hearts and repent of any racism still lurking there."

A good argument, I thought, but my article never made it to press. Perhaps it's too uncomfortable for Adventists to admit that we might have prejudice in our own ranks.

Right here I should note the difference between prejudice and racism, as explained to me by a Hispanic leader in the North American Division. "Prejudice," he said, "is a predisposition to dislike someone of another race. It is rooted in ignorance; often an enlightening interracial encounter will transform one's outlook and attitude. Racism, however, is determined hatred based on nothing more significant than skin color or cultural customs. It is wickedness of the heart that no amount of mere information can remove."

The sad fact is that both prejudice and racism have slithered under the doors of some Adventist churches, at times even coiling behind our pulpits. You might question my assessment if you have the same color of skin I have. But when you take the time for a heart-to-heart talk with a veteran black or Hispanic church leader, what you hear may bring you surprise and grief. Several I have spoken with have baptized more souls than I ever will if I live to last a century. These leaders have a right to be heard. But they face a dilemma. If they speak out, it appears they have an attitude problem. Yet if they keep quiet and try to be team players, they worry about betraying their racial heritage. So most of them have learned to pray a lot, entrusting everything to the Judge of all the earth. Thank God, people are praying, but we must also work together in Christ's name to confront the demons of racism.

Some expressions of racism in Adventist history are simply shocking. The book *We Have Tomorrow* recounts a tragic incident that happened at one of our hospitals in the early 1940s. Lucy Byard, a black Adventist, was critically ill with pneumonia. "Fair-skinned, at first she was admitted, but later when admittance forms were scrutinized and her racial identity discovered, she was told a mistake had been made. Without examination or treatment she was wheeled out into the corridor"[3] with her life hanging in the balance. Someone finally rescued her and took her to a non-Adventist hospital willing to offer a black person the ministry of healing. But that faithful Adventist sister died, needlessly, because her treatment was delayed. What killed her? Adventist racism.

We could discuss numerous other examples of heartbreaking prejudice and racism in Adventist institutions and churches, some of which are chronicled in the eye-opening book *Righteous Rebel* by W. W. Fordham.[4] If you've ever wondered why Christ as yet has been unable to finish His work through our church, I suggest you read Elder Fordham's book, along with *We Have Tomorrow* by Louis B. Reynolds. You might conclude that the "good old days" weren't all that good. No wonder generation after generation has perished while wandering in the wilderness of racism and legalism. I'm afraid that many vegetarian, tithe-paying, Sabbath-keeping racists will wake up a thousand years too late! Anticipating a "well done" affirmation from Christ, they will instead hear His sentence of doom: "Inasmuch as you did it to one of the least of these My brethren, you did it to Me. . . . Depart from Me, you cursed" (Matthew 25:40, 41).

Is that too harsh an assessment of racism? Perhaps not, when we consider that "the inhumanity of man toward man is our greatest sin."[5]

Thank God, things are changing in our church. We've come a long way in overcoming racism. But have we come far enough?

Where we still fall short

Specifically, where might Seventh-day Adventists still be falling short? I think one example is the tendency of some white members to blame any problems experienced by minority leaders upon the color of their skin. If a black or Hispanic administrator makes a financial misjudgment, it automatically becomes a racial issue. If a minister stumbles into immorality, people give credence to other racial stereotypes. All this amounts to prejudice and racism.

Another blatant example is the way we sometimes shun inter-racial couples. In one church I served, a mixed-race couple who ventured through the door were treated as though they were Willie Horton with Typhoid Mary. How sad.

Frankly, I can't encourage people of different races to marry; I know that beyond the challenge of achieving cultural compatibility, the couple will suffer society's continual frown. Prospects for a happy marriage are not encouraging. Furthermore, children from interracial marriages may find themselves alienated from both races. Not being black or white, they often must struggle within themselves to discover their identity.

Despite the truth in all that, when interracial partners risk the odds and get married, every Christian ought to welcome them into full fellowship and hospitality. If you don't think so, then tell me where in the Bible do you find support for refusing fellowship to an interracial man and wife? On what basis can we regard cross-cultural marriage as a moral or spiritual problem? Paul's passage about being unequally yoked addresses wedlock between believers and unbelievers, not interracial relations. The only moral mandate that I know of regarding one's choice of a marriage partner is that we should respect the individual's freedom of choice and receive one another as Christ has received us. If we refuse these Christian responsibilities, prejudice and racism may be lurking in our hearts.

I have a personal confession to make. Before coming to terms with this position on interracial marriages, I would feel offended when I saw a black man keeping company with a white woman— or vice versa. Now I realize that the Lord hasn't called me to impose my convictions—or my prejudices and insecurities—upon their freedom to associate with whomever they please. If they ask my opinion, I can express my reservations. Otherwise, I should keep my mouth closed and my heart open to them.

There are other examples of racial shortcomings in the Christian community, most of them subtle. For example, many minority leaders believe church organizations have a glass ceiling above which they cannot be "promoted" except in token instances. Church administrators with whom I've discussed this express frustration, believing they are already working hard to achieve proportionate minority representation in leadership. Adventist churches around the world have made dramatic progress in equal-opportunity employment for black, Hispanic, and Asian leaders. We need more. At present in North America, Hispanics, especially, find themselves on the short end of proportionate leadership representation in the Adventist Church.[6]

Another example of prejudice and racism is difficult to prove, but it's real nonetheless. You know how during the days of slavery plantation owners expected blacks to work in the fields while they attended management matters. Well, some whites today still display a plantation mentality in expecting minorities to reap the fields of evangelism while Anglos oversee the work of God and perhaps pursue doctorates in prestigious ministries such as counseling. Not surprisingly, membership growth has stalled for Anglo Adventists in North America while Hispanic, black, and Asian baptisms are flourishing.

But it seems to me that the greatest example of racism in the Adventist Church is the low priority we assign to it on the totem pole of sins to avoid. Most of us seem to regard racial hatred (when we become aware of it) as more of a social misdemeanor than a spiritual felony, forgetting that "the inhumanity of man toward man is our greatest sin."

Overcoming racism

How can we rid ourselves of prejudice and racism? We must transcend our obsession with depersonalized doctrine and begin to really value people. Truth itself is a person—the Lord Jesus Christ (see John 14:6). He waged war against racism sponsored by the religious establishment of His day, shocking friends and foes alike by extending His love to the despised Gentiles. Today it remains true that only the warm love of His gospel can cleanse the proud heart of racial hatred. "He Himself is our peace, who has made both one, and has broken down the middle wall of division between us" (Ephesians 2:14). "Therefore receive one another, just as Christ also received us, to the glory of God" (Romans 15:7).

According to the Bible, this love toward one another is "the fulfillment of the law" (Romans 13:10). Thus sin, the breaking of the law, involves more than the violation of a written code. Actually, evildoing is basically a violation of relationships. Sin isn't wrong because of the pleasure it promises the indulger. Sin is sin because it destroys our relationships by ruining our capacity to love and be loved.

Take tobacco, for example. Smoking is bad because it threatens my body, which is God's temple and His instrument to serve people. Since racism causes greater harm to my relationships than addiction to tobacco, it is a more serious sin. Hatred toward my brother or sister creates smoke in God's nostrils worse than a stinking cigar.

We hate tobacco because it causes cancer. But racism *is* cancer. It's a malignant curse, even in the church.

Reverse racism

Although some individuals would disagree, white people aren't the only perpetrators of prejudice. Some blacks, regarding racism as the abuse of social and economic power, feel that because whites are the only ones with such power, only they can qualify as racist. In reality, victims of any kind of abuse frequently learn to emulate the behavior they have suffered. Molested children often themselves become molesters, and victims of racism often themselves become racists. I'm thinking of Sister Souljah, whose comments about killing white people certainly reflected racism. We have seen faces of all colors reflecting similar racial hatred; Sister Souljah has many cousins.

Reverse racism exists even in the church. When a black worker deserves discipline, some peers will accuse white leadership of racism or prejudice. If funds cannot be found for their projects, some blacks automatically attribute the "No" vote to white racism. Minorities sometimes expect preferential treatment, and if they don't get it, they become embittered. Some seem determined to mistrust anyone with a white face. Again, how sad.

For the most part, the faith of black Christians helps them restrain the racist resentment expressed by many secular African-Americans. Much black rap music, or "hip hop," simmers with hatred against white power. Particularly vicious are the songs of Ice-T and those of Sister Souljah's mentor, Chuck D. Has the thought occurred to these rap singers that it might be beneficial for black youth to trade in their knives and guns for the education needed to triumph over white racism? Other despised minorities manage to make it.

Consider Asian immigrants. When Korean and Japanese immigrants pass through customs at Los Angeles International

Airport, the KKK isn't waiting with a welcome wagon serving cookies and milk. Despite intimidating obstacles that include a language barrier, many Asians in America manage to survive and thrive. Japanese-Americans, who suffered racial imprisonment during World War II, have soared to the heights of economic success by means of education and discipline. So have the Koreans. Instead of burning out Korean businesses, those who participated in the Los Angeles riots would do well to emulate whatever it is that makes Asians succeed despite the odds stacked against them.

We must acknowledge, of course, that Asians came here without their hands tied behind their backs, free to pursue the American dream. Africans were coerced to come here as slaves. Blacks have had to overcome centuries of bondage, not just to white power but to the lie that they cannot succeed. The resulting self-doubt—and in some cases self-hatred—is a daunting and unrelenting challenge.

Nevertheless, millions of African-Americans have conquered white racism and their own poverty through education, discipline, and determination. Unfortunately, even after they have made it to the top and have proven themselves in every way, they still face continuing character scrutiny on the basis of their skin color. Most of them learn to shrug it off or even laugh about it; prejudice is so irrational it can be ridiculous. Sadly, however, the ongoing struggle is too much for some black people to cope with. They just give up trying to make something of their lives, becoming hopeless and sometimes violent. Mostly just hopeless.

The price of hopelessness

I think of a black man in his twenties whom I met at the Exxon station on my lunch break the other day. Tall and thin, he hesitantly approached my car asking if I had a dollar for bus fare so he could get to the shopping plaza up the road. "Hop in," I invited him, "and I'll take you there." As we drove along he told me of his struggles to support his wife and daughter. He had been laid off his construction job and hoped to get work at the supermarket. He didn't know the manager, and neither did I, but I went inside with him, thinking that putting in a good word for him might increase his odds of getting a job. The manager was polite but had nothing to offer. The young man's shoulders sagged. How would he support his family? I helped him buy some groceries and prayed with him. That's all I could do. Then we parted.

Watching him go his way, I realized how easy it is for many men of his race to fall into the traps of low self-esteem, hopelessness, bitterness, and finally violence. Beyond all this, a tradition of female home leadership endures from the days of forced separation in slavery, and it remains for many black men to rediscover their role in the family circle.

Sports has been a mixed blessing for black men. On one hand, it provides a level playing field to compete man to man against whites. On the other hand, a career in sports is numerically possible only for a select few. The success of blacks in sports also fuels the stereotype that blacks have physical prowess while whites have superior mental skills.

Rather than glorifying blacks who have managed to make it in sports and entertainment, we need to highlight the many black successes in business, education, and the professions. Jesse Jackson, for example, emerged from a sharecropper's house to campaign for the White House. And my friend Benjamin Carson, a young Seventh-day Adventist neurosurgeon, rose from a glass-strewn ghetto in Detroit to the heights of medical achievement and service to humanity. Another Adventist, Eva B. Dykes, became the first black woman ever to earn a doctoral degree.

Many other African-Americans deserve mention, spiritual giants who have contributed far more than their share to the outreach and nurture of church members in North America, both black and white: C. D. Brooks, E. E. Cleveland, C. E. Bradford, C. E. Dudley, Calvin Rock, Eric Ward, Walter Pearson, Jr., William Scales, Jr., and others too numerous to mention. It is through their faithful leadership that black Adventists have largely escaped the snares of certain destructive and legalistic organizations that are ravaging white members. Seldom if ever do you hear of heresies running loose in the African-American Adventist community. Hispanic leaders are also effective in tending to the needs of their flock.

The success of these leaders testifies how faith, love, and dedicated discipline can overcome all obstacles. Minority Americans everywhere must also rise up and walk. The same skills that some are abusing as successful drug dealers, others are profitably employing in civic or spiritual leadership or in a legitimate business.

While society doesn't owe anyone a living, it does owe everyone an opportunity. Without jobs available, inner-city youth—blacks, Hispanics, and whites alike—find it easy to lapse into careers in crime and selling drugs. I believe our government must provide millions of additional dollars in small business grants and loans. Enterprise zones, properly administrated, will encourage billions of dollars of business investment in minority communities.

Although corporate and government funding—and lots of it—is needed to foster employment and educational opportunities, let's remember that money alone won't cure the bankruptcy of values that plagues the ghetto. Uncle Sam can't pretend to be Santa Claus. Hasn't the welfare money tree often yielded the fruit of irresponsible behavior?

Society's stairway to success may be far steeper for minority youth, but the door at the top has been cracked open. There's a new world of opportunity waiting through education, diligence, and—most of all—faith in God's personal providence. No David Duke on earth can frustrate heaven's ultimate plan for one's personal life. If God is for minorities, who can be against them?

The devil may detain you, but he need not derail you. Racism may harass, but it need not triumph.

Red people

What a witness this world would have if believers of all colors and cultures would humble their hearts and love one another as Christ has loved us!

In November 1992 the South African Union invited me to hold meetings there. I was eager to go in support of the recent decision to abolish denominational apartheid. One Sabbath, in the beautiful coastal city of East London, I spoke at one of the first interracial convocations ever held there. Looking at the sea of multiracial faces scattered throughout the auditorium, I ventured a prediction. I told the audience that God won't allow any black people in heaven. As black, white, and colored faces registered shock at such unexpected arrogance, I quickly added that there won't be any white people up there either. That eased the tension somewhat, but left them even more perplexed. "Praise the Lord," I concluded, "the only ones going to heaven will be red people, washed in the blood of the Lamb."

Actually, I'm looking forward to fellowship in heaven with black saints as well as those who are white, yellow, red, and brown. Our God, who delights in the many colors of flowers, also takes pride in the many races and cultures from every tribe and nation that comprise the rainbow of His human family.

Blacks, whites, Hispanics, and Asians are all different, just as in a choir the basses, sopranos, tenors, and altos are different— yet they manage to sing the same song in harmony. If we start celebrating each other's distinctiveness now, we will be prepared to continue that fellowship in heaven.

I thank God for my mother, whose uncle in Germany during World War II risked death from a SS firing squad to help some Jewish prisoners escape execution. My father also taught me that Yahweh, the God of heaven, created all of us equal in His sight. The Lord has helped me overcome much of my own prejudice, although from time to time the dragon of intolerance still roars within me.

Let me take you back to Hawaii, where we started this chapter. While there for the first time on a speaking appointment, I drove along the coast west of Honolulu to Pearl Harbor—site of the unprovoked Japanese attack that sparked America's involvement in World War II. In the visitors' center I viewed with horror a movie of those bombers from the land of the rising sun diving down from the blue sky with their payloads of death. Anger swirled within me as I noticed a group of Japanese tourists in the front row attentively viewing the film.

What are they doing here? I grumbled silently. *I'll bet they're proud of what their parents did to the U.S. Navy.*

I kept a wary eye on those foreigners as we all boarded the boat to the *Arizona* Memorial. When we reached the spot where more than a thousand American sailors lie entombed in the murky, oil-fouled depths, all my prejudice suddenly floated away.

Why? It was the sight of those Japanese tourists, one by one, removing the flowered leis from their necks and reverently dropping them into the harbor. It was a profound and touching expression of regret for the death of their former enemies. As thirty-one circles of yellow, white, and red drifted away with the morning tide, it was my turn to feel regret. Those floating halos of flowers carried with them all my prejudice toward Japanese people.

Wouldn't it be wonderful if we Adventists would remove our necklaces of racial disharmony and drop them at the feet of Jesus? Racial conflict will float away in the blood shed on the cross. Then our Christian neighbors will gain new respect for us as fellow members of God's multicultural family.

---

1. Norman K. Miles, "Tension Between the Races," in *The World of Ellen G. White*, ed. Gary Land (Washington, D.C.: Review & Herald, 1987), 50.

2. Ibid., 54.

3. Louis B. Reynolds, *We Have Tomorrow* (Washington, D.C.: Review & Herald, 1984), 293.

4. W. W. Fordham, *Righteous Rebel* (Washington, D.C.: Review & Herald, 1990).

5. Ellen G. White, *The Ministry of Healing* (Mountain View, Calif.: Pacific Press, 1942), 163.

6. See Manual Vasquez, *America's Changing Face and the Church's Changing Voice* (Silver Spring, Md.: North American Division of Seventh-day Adventists, 1992).

Chapter 4

Pro-Life or Pro-Choice?

(Abortion)

Palm Springs, California, is the scene of spring break madness for thousands of West Coast college students. During Holy Week of 1989, police had their hands full, dealing with drunkenness, nudity, and unrelenting revelry. More than a thousand students were arrested before order was restored in that desert community.

Meanwhile, 110 miles away in Los Angeles, an equal number of people also found themselves in jail. Not for drinking or carousing; these were praying, singing Christians, crusading against the loss of babies through abortion.

Is there anything else that so divides our society as the abortion debate? Those who plead for the survival of the unborn call themselves pro-life, while those who defend the rights of women to control their own bodies proclaim themselves pro-choice. Pro-life or pro-choice? That is the question. Many consider the answer to be the greatest moral issue of our time. We must come to terms with it in these pages as we wrestle with reality.

Even Seventh-day Adventists find themselves struggling on opposite ends of a desperate tug-of-war. We value life as God's sacred gift, but we also treasure religious liberty with its freedom of conscience. Can we possibly have it both ways? That is, can we be *both* pro-life and pro-choice? I think you will see that we can, in a quiet, thoughtful spirit of Christian understanding.

The abortive lifestyle

There's more here than first meets the mind. Abortion involves more than an act of terminating pregnancy; for many in our society it has become the preferred lifestyle, the way they cope with any problem that comes their way. Is there trouble at school? Don't bother to study harder; just abort your education. That's the take-it-easy attitude many have today. Are you having problems at work? Quit. Abort your job. Has holy wedlock become unhappy deadlock? Divorce. Get an abortion from your vows. Are you faltering in your Christian experience? Take the easy way out and abort your religious experience.

In many cases, aborting a pregnancy shares this same mind-set of escapism. Those who regard abortion as a form of belated birth control belie a truth of Scripture clearly taught from Genesis to Revelation: "Do not be deceived, God is not mocked; for whatever a man sows, that he will also reap. For he who sows to his flesh will of the flesh reap corruption" (Galatians 6:7, 8).

Although conception requires male participation, unless a woman has the support of a loving husband, she often faces childbirth all alone. Many find the pressures of pregnancy too much to bear alone, and reluctantly they opt for an abortion. As understandable as such a decision may be, abortion is not God's solution to the predicament. For better or worse, the Bible says we will reap the consequences of our actions. Abortion as birth control attempts to escape this fundamental fact of life; the tragic result is that a human heart stops beating.

Consider the case of a popular, fun-loving teenager who belonged to a church I once served as pastor. Let's call her Jennifer. Her pursuit of happiness got her pregnant. The solution seemed simple enough to her parents: Get her off the hook (and save their reputation) with an abortion. Why should the family have to suffer through a disruptive and embarrassing pregnancy?

Getting an abortion is always a traumatic event in itself—a reality that escapes many pro-life activists. The fact remains, however, that the instant cancellation of a pregnancy appears to provide the quickest, easiest route back to normalcy. That's why Jennifer and her parents opted for it, they told me later.

Unfortunately, having aborted her problem, Jennifer never

learned her lesson. Next summer she got pregnant again. And again after that. Four abortions before the age of twenty-one, believe it or not. The pregnancies weren't her fault alone, of course. The primary blame probably rested with the good-time Charlies who wanted a night of fun but not the responsibilities of fatherhood. Without support from them or from church members, Jennifer simply stopped attending services. When I arrived as her new pastor, she had aborted Christianity, believing that all religion consisted only of strict standards without compensating love or mercy.

I wonder what would have happened if Jennifer had known the love of Jesus through the members of the church? She might not have attempted to escape reality with that first abortion. Nine months of pregnancy would have been tough, but encouraged by the grace of God, she could have accepted one of life's most important lessons: We must bear the consequences of our actions.

Christian values vs. humanism

The twisted value system of this world rejects God's principle of reaping what we sow. In many other ways society's values are in shambles. Consider the apathy toward what is growing in the womb. An unborn baby is regarded as the moral equivalent of a tumor—discard "it" if you choose, no questions asked. But suppose it were a little dolphin swimming around inside of a pregnant mother. You can be sure that Hollywood's save-the-dolphin protesters would furiously defend its right to life. Doesn't it seem strange that the same activists who are so militant about preserving every dolphin in the ocean don't show equal concern for humanity in the womb?

When the state of California decided to finally execute a condemned murderer, crowds holding candlelight vigils camped outside the death chamber of the state prison. Yet many of these same people condemn those who hold similar protests outside the death chambers of abortion clinics. Celebrities from Hollywood campaign with equal fervor for the preservation of convicted murderers and the privilege of killing unborn babies. Their motives may be sincere, but their logic isn't easy to follow.

All this seems strange, doesn't it? Such is the religion of secular humanism.

Christianity, on the other hand, values life as a gift from God—a gift so sacred that He sacrificed His own life to preserve it. *The bottom line for Christians, then, is whether an unborn child is really alive.* If it is a living human being, we must ask the question: What has that baby done to deserve death?

Viability and personhood

You may be thinking that an unborn baby isn't really alive because it isn't breathing. Well, if it doesn't have life, then why does it have a beating heart? And if it isn't a human being, what kind of being is it? If it isn't a child, why is it sucking its thumb?

But isn't it necessary for a living being to have the breath of life? In reality, a baby in the womb is just as much a consumer of oxygen as anyone else. Yes, mother's help is needed to process that life-sustaining air, but many adults undergoing surgery also need help breathing. Without that respirator they would die. Do they cease being humans during their operation because they cannot breathe on their own?

Even after a baby is born and can begin breathing, it still isn't fully "viable," that is, capable of living on its own. It can't feed itself, support itself financially, or even roll over in its crib. Obviously, viability has nothing to do with personhood.

Consider also the elderly and the severely handicapped who cannot live on their own. Does that mean they aren't real people? This type of thinking gave birth to Hitler's "final solution." The Nazis considered helpless members of society to be expendable "useless eaters." Some thoughtful minds ponder the staggering cost of thirty million unborn lives and worry whether a new holocaust is happening right now, right here in America.

We can debate about exactly when life begins, but shouldn't the burden of proof belong to those who would invade the womb and terminate that life? Obviously a short trip down the birth canal does not convert a depersonalized fetus into a human being—life must begin sometime before birth. Some point to the passage from one trimester to another, but no magical transformation takes place from one division of time to the next. The most natural, logical position is that life begins at conception. From that instant onward there is continuous growth and maturing.

Remember that an unborn baby has all the indications of humanity well within the first trimester of life. He or she has a perfectly formed body with organs functioning. About the twenty-first day after conception—even before the mother may know she is pregnant—the heart of her baby is already pumping blood. Unborn babies have amazing capabilities that medical science is just now beginning to appreciate. They already have their own personalities. They can recognize the voice of their mothers, who, in turn, are bonded to that life within the womb. When a mother violates the unwritten law of maternal instinct by aborting her baby, no wonder she often feels nagging guilt for years to come for ending a human life.

In their compassion for women who get abortions, pro-choice advocates go to great lengths to deny that abortions kill human beings. For example, one church policy statement on abortion refers to it as the "interruption" of pregnancy—as if John Wilkes Booth merely interrupted the presidency of Abraham Lincoln!

The Bible and the unborn

We who are Christians should be interested to know what the Bible says about the unborn. We read that the virgin Mary was "with *child* of the Holy Spirit" (Matthew 1:18, emphasis supplied). The eternal Lord was a real, living child inside Mary's womb. Think about this: If unborn babies are not living beings, where was Jesus while Mary was pregnant? Did He cease to exist for nine months?

In a number of places, the Bible refers to unborn babies as people. For example, when Christ's aunt Elizabeth met His mother Mary: "Indeed, as soon as the voice of your greeting sounded in my ears, the babe leaped in my womb for joy" (Luke 1:44). According to the Bible, what Elizabeth carried inside her womb was a baby. Not a mass of developing fetal tissue, but a bouncing baby boy. In the light of both biological and scriptural evidence, can we possibly escape the conviction that abortion terminates human life? And what right do we have to stop that precious beating heart?

Scripture explicitly defends the rights of the unborn. If an assailant in Old Testament times struck a woman and caused her to give birth prematurely, he was fined. But if that unborn life was lost, the sentence was death: "You shall appoint as a penalty life for life" (Exodus 21:23, NASB).[1]

Many atheists and agnostics lack true respect for human life. To them, an unborn baby may be just fetal tissue evolving in the womb—a symbol of the evolutionary process. Such a denial of life that God has granted violates the sixth commandment. Also the fourth, since the Sabbath commandment requires respect for created life. Abortion, by sabotaging God's life in the womb, undermines the Sabbath.

Jesus said of Himself: "The Son gives life to whom he is pleased to give it" (John 5:21, NIV). He also declared: "I hold the keys of death" (Revelation 1:18, NIV). Abortion empowers mere mortals to become the lords of life or death, playing the role of God. It therefore receives its authority from the one who said, "Ye shall be as gods" (Genesis 3:5, KJV). Is it possible that those who defend abortion, well-meaning though they may be, actually promote the work of the devil? That would be tragic and most regrettable.

Feminists of the radical type warn, "Get your hands off my body!" Well, if God has seen fit to grant life to those babies in the womb, shouldn't we get our hands off *their* little bodies?

Of all parties involved when abortion is considered, no one is more helpless or threatened than the unborn child. In our age of violent solutions to the problems of the world, the church is called to protect the helpless, the endangered, and the unwanted. As members of the human family, we ourselves were helpless and endangered after Adam sinned. God might have saved Himself a lot of trouble by aborting us. Instead, at great expense and embarrassment on the cross, He opted for adoption.

Aren't you glad He did? Shouldn't we go and do likewise?

Defending human choice

I think you will agree that there's quite a compelling case for being pro-life, but what about the other side of the coin, human choice? Can we be pro-choice as well as pro-life?

God has indeed given us freedom of individual conscience (see

2 Corinthians 3:17). However, He expects us to make responsible choices: "I have set before you life and death, blessings and curses. Now choose life, so that you and your children may live" (Deuteronomy 30:19, NIV). When Adam and Eve exercised their power of choice and committed sin, death came to the human family. Still today the well-being of children—including the unborn—depends upon right choices by parents. Some suggest that since abortion is one of the tragic dilemmas of human fallenness, decisions about life must be made in the context of a fallen world. What is this supposed to mean? It's all right to disobey God when the going gets tough? Is this the lesson from Daniel in the lion's den? The three young Hebrews in the fiery furnace? Or Jesus sweating blood in Gethsemane?

Nothing in the Bible suggests that God ever lowers His standards to suit difficult circumstances. Instead, He gives strength to meet the test. If we start making allowances for committing abortion because of the tragic dilemma of human fallenness, the next thing you know we'll be finding excuses for smoking, Sabbath breaking, withholding tithe, and even adultery. Such thinking is extremely dangerous and presents to God an offering of strange fire.

We are in the last days of earth's history, about to suffer a time of trouble such as never was. Despite a worldwide economic boycott and a death decree, the final remnant will courageously keep the commandments of God and the faith of Jesus. There will be no compromises and no excuses, even in that context of a very fallen world.

Unlimited freedom?

When those who are committed to obey God stumble and fall, He has mercy on them, but He cannot justify deliberate, calculated disregard of His commandments. Furthermore, He expects responsible Christians to take responsibility for their choices.

When a man and a woman, married or not, willingly engage in sexual intercourse, they have also chosen to enter into risk that a baby may result. A man then assumes the possibility of fatherhood, with all the associated responsibilities to which he must be held accountable. Likewise, a woman who has chosen to have sex has also exercised her freedom of choice about conceiving human life.

There is no such thing as unlimited freedom of choice; personal freedom cannot violate another individual's rights. Thus a woman's right over her body ends where her baby's body begins. The fact that an unborn baby can't defend itself doesn't mean it has no rights.

But what about pregnancies from rape and incest? Such cases deserve special consideration, since the mother never had an opportunity to exercise her legitimate free choice. Why should she be forced to face the consequences of someone else's crime? Because of this, many who normally oppose abortion approve such an option in cases of forced pregnancy. Since the mother was impregnated without her choice, wouldn't she have the right to defend herself against that intrusion? Why must she reap what she didn't sow?

And what about performing an abortion to save the life of the mother? Such cases are relatively rare, but occasionally doctors find themselves faced with the terrible dilemma of deciding whether mother or child should live—or possibly losing both lives if an abortion is not performed. In such situations abortion may be justified to prevent the greater tragedy.

At this point we must venture into an especially delicate area. What if the unborn baby is genetically crippled? Often in such cases the mother's body deals with the crisis by causing a miscarriage. But suppose God allows the baby to develop—are we able to decide whether that person's quality of life will be worth the trouble of coping with a handicap? Many handicapped people enjoy profoundly fulfilling lives. You may know that the composer Beethoven suffered such congenital defects that some twentieth-century doctors might have wanted to abort him. Music lovers everywhere can be glad that Beethoven's mother didn't.

I know we are tiptoeing through some delicate and controversial questions here. A strong case can be made that life is so sacred that no human has the right to choose abortion under any circumstances. Some answers don't come easy, but while we wonder what should be done in cases of rape, incest, genetic disability, and saving the life of the mother, let's do something now about the vast majority of abortions in which a healthy mother rids herself of a healthy baby that exists by her own free choice. We could immediately relieve society of the burden of the vast majority of its abortions. Having accomplished that, we could continue to discuss the ethics of abortion in those questionable situations.

Loving options

Well, those are my convictions about abortion. I wish you could know how I have agonized over this chapter. Some would be skeptical of my motives, denouncing anyone who has pro-life convictions as being heartless. Many feminists deny men the right to speak out against abortion, since only a woman can know what it's like to be pregnant. Yet these same activists lecture confidently about men and why they commit violence. How do they know what goes on inside a man's mind? Do we have a double standard here?

The fact is that all of us, men and women, have not only a right but a responsibility to express our moral convictions in a respectful and loving way. Perhaps you feel I haven't been sensitive enough. Please remember that the matter under discussion is not how sensitive I happen to be but whether there is human life in the womb. Nevertheless, please also believe me that, having been a pastor, I know something of the anguish women suffer when they consider an abortion. They need compassion, not condemnation, whatever they decide to do. And if they do make the courageous choice of preserving that life within them, the crisis isn't over—it has only just begun. They need help in bringing their babies into the world and pulling their own lives back together. The church has a solemn duty to stand by their side.

An Adventist layperson in California, George Lawson, has launched Loving Options, a ministry for women in crisis pregnancy. Qualified Christian professionals volunteer their time at the clinic, offering counseling and medical services to pregnant women willing to consider options other than abortion for their pregnancy.[2] I wish Loving Options would have been there twelve years ago to help Jennifer, that troubled young woman whose pastor I used to be. Along with medical services and other assistance, Loving Options would have provided spiritual encouragement. Jennifer would have heard from them something like this:

"Jennifer, please understand that God loves you despite your mistakes. He has a special plan for your life—and for the life of that little baby inside you. You might not be able to provide a home for your baby, but many childless couples are praying every night before an empty bassinet. By entrusting your baby to their care, you can turn your own nightmare into the fulfillment of their fondest dreams.

"Perhaps you feel guilty about the abortions you've already had. Just confess your sin to Jesus and claim His gift of forgiveness. Actually, we are all guilty of sin and deserving of death. The Bible says that all of us, like sheep, have gone astray, each of us has turned to his own way. But thank God, at the cross He laid upon Jesus the iniquity of us all.

"Yes, Jennifer, Jesus paid the full price of our salvation. Now we can stand clean before God, just as if we had never done anything wrong. Just as if we've always done everything perfectly! And the Lord not only forgives us and counts us perfect; He also gives us a new life full of wholesome, positive relationships."

I wish I could report that Jennifer immediately came back to Jesus and the church. By now, maybe she has. If not, then someday, with the support of her sisters and brothers in Christ, I believe she will rejoice in His love and forgiveness. All of us need mercy from God more than we can know, and we all need to share it with each other.

---

1. Defenders of abortion attempt to prove from Exodus 21 that the fetus in the womb is inferior to human life. I believe that an unbiased analysis of the Hebrew text proves otherwise. Evidence I found persuasive is in the *Ministry* article by Ron du Preez, "The Fetus in Biblical Law" (September 1992).

If one disagrees with this interpretation of Exodus 21:22-25, the fact remains that we cannot determine personhood by whether or not the death penalty exists for killing that life. Notice a verse immediately preceding our passage (verse 20), in which someone who kills a slave is not put to death but merely punished. Nobody in today's society would deny that a slave is a human being—yet the Bible doesn't enforce the death penalty for killing a slave.

2. Loving Options is a nonprofit crisis pregnancy ministry. This group's newsletter is available by writing 24769 Redlands Blvd., Suite E, San Bernardino, CA 92408. If you write to George Lawson, you may wish to ask for information about another nonprofit organization of which he is a member, "Adventists for Life."

Chapter 5

Liberty Must Have Limits

(Legislating morality)

"Personally, I'm pro-life," one of my friends declared, "but when it comes to abortion legislation, I'm pro-choice. I don't want to impose my convictions upon society. After all, you can't legislate morality."

Is it really true that human government cannot legislate morality? We hear it all the time, and for years I believed it myself. I don't anymore.

Please let me explain why. I don't expect you to agree with everything you read in this chapter. Like everything else in this book, legislating morality is controversial. Honest citizens, even faithful Adventists, fervently disagree about what should be the law of the land and what should be left up to personal conscience. This is my attempt to contribute to the ongoing discussion.

Caesar's responsibility

Imagine the anarchy in our land if civil morality were not legislated and enforced. Society couldn't survive! No man would be safe from being murdered; no woman would have a refuge from rapists; no baby could rest secure from the risk of being kidnapped or aborted.

For the common good of all citizens, the Constitution of the United States and the basic charters of other civilized nations safeguard life, liberty, and the pursuit of happiness. Those who favor abortion rights are enthusiastic about preserving personal liberty and the pursuit of happiness, but they fail to protect life in the womb.

"Keep your convictions to yourself," they say. "Don't try to legislate morality." They forget that society needs law and order—civil morality. When it comes to religious morality, however, we must draw a line in the legislative sand. The Bible itself distinguishes between our civil responsibility to government and our personal religious obligation to God. Jesus said: "Render therefore to Caesar the things that are Caesar's, and to God the things that are God's" (Matthew 22:21). So we must keep separate those things that belong to Caesar (civil government) from those things that belong to God (religious matters).

The Ten Commandments given to Moses in Old Testament times show these same two elements. Commandments pertaining to one's relationship with God cannot be enforced by human government. But those relating to citizenship—"Thou shalt not kill," for example—are essential in any society to preserve law and order. These commandments the state must uphold by whatever means necessary to protect life and property. And since unborn babies are living human beings, they are entitled to the same protection as any other member of society. This requires the legislation of civil morality.

Prayer that's not OK

When it comes to religion, however, government must protect the free expression of faith but not promote it. Yes, it would be wonderful if everybody would voluntarily choose to believe in God and accept biblical morality. But whose interpretation of the Bible? That's the question.

A while back the state legislature in California had a Buddhist chaplain. Christians didn't appreciate having their tax dollars sponsoring what they considered to be pagan prayers. Likewise, Buddhists, Muslims, Jews, and atheists aren't happy that the United States Senate appoints a Christian chaplain to offer prayer in the national legislative chambers. Any type of government-sponsored chaplaincy that favors one religion over another is inappropriate.

What about school prayer? Certainly, children should pray everywhere, including in school. But who should teach them to pray? Do we want Catholic prayers? Protestant prayers? Jewish prayers? Hindu or Muslim prayers?

When government gets into the business of sponsoring prayer, some citizens always find themselves left out. That's why Uncle Sam should avoid all temptation to promote religious behavior—and why we Adventists need to maintain our own parochial school system.

Public prayer that may be OK

Not all church members can send their children to Adventist schools. In such cases, our young people can counter the secular environment by initiating prayer and fellowship groups for fellow students. Their religious activities are perfectly legal as long as the school itself doesn't sponsor them or get involved. And that's how it ought to be, don't you think? If the students want to pray by themselves, Uncle Sam should forbid them not.

Is there any occasion where prayer or religious testimony is appropriate at an official public-school function? Suppose a student earns the right to make a speech because of some personal achievement, such as becoming the class valedictorian? Consider the case of Angela Guidry. She wanted to include a few sentences in her valedictory speech thanking God for her scholastic achievements. The Louisiana teenager felt it would be wrong to accept the honor without giving Him the glory. The principal, however, denied her right of free speech, not wanting her audience to be exposed to partisan religious influences. Did he do the right thing?

Absolutely not, in my opinion. While it would have been improper for the school to arrange for prayer or religious testimony, Angela had earned the right to compose her own speech and say whatever she pleased within the bounds of respect and decency. Had school officials permitted her testimony, they wouldn't have been showing religious preference. State-sponsored religion was not the issue.

The principal may have meant well, but he robbed that young woman of a once-in-a-lifetime opportunity for which she had studied so hard. Rather than accepting human honor without giving glory to God, Angela decided to forgo her speech entirely. To me, she suffered an inexcusable obstruction of her personal religious liberty and her freedom of speech.

Now, suppose the captain of the football team is expected to address fellow teammates or spectators before a game, and he wants to offer public prayer. Is that OK? I think so. The school would have no business *appointing* someone to pray; that would be religious favoritism on behalf of whomever they appointed. But if a student qualifies himself through some personal achievement to make a speech—and he wants that speech to be a prayer—why should the school have a right to suppress that person's privilege of free speech?

Peril of government-sponsored religion

Having affirmed what I consider to be legitimate public prayer and testimony, I'd like to say again that government itself should not sponsor religious expression. That could lead to other intrusions into the sacred circle of personal faith, resulting ultimately in persecution.

Many imagine that it's fine if the government sponsors religious faith in general as long as it doesn't favor one particular religion. In this view, separation of church and state merely forbids a state-sponsored denomination. This may seem reasonable at first, but an experiment of this type long ago in the American colonies bore disastrous results. The state of Maryland, where I live, was founded primarily as a refuge for persecuted Catholics, although Christians of all faiths were welcome. The Maryland assembly in 1649 proclaimed an "Act of Toleration," which provided that all who confess Jesus would be accepted as citizens. Yet even this so-called "Act of Toleration," as sincere as it was, inspired religious persecution. No liberty, for example, was offered to non-Christians. And even fellow Christians who disbelieved a particular doctrine, such as the Trinity, found themselves ticketed for the death penalty.

Persecution naturally results when faith becomes law—even when nondenominational faith is enforced. God Himself will not force faith. Why then should we? But civil morality, which protects the rights of fellow human beings—born and unborn—deserves the full support of all citizens and organizations, including the church.

Dreadful decisions

Back in the 1850s the U.S. Supreme Court decreed in the Dred Scott decision that African-Americans were not fully human—that they were property without the rights accorded to other human beings. Many professed Christians actually supported that damnable legal pronouncement. Others disagreed yet refused to join the crusade for abolition of slavery. Perhaps they didn't wish to get entangled in legislating morality, even though human lives were being violated by slavery.

In 1973 the Supreme Court again denied the reality of humanity in *Roe vs. Wade*. And once again many Christians are keeping quiet, not wanting to get involved in what they regard as a political debate. They seem to overlook the reality that helpless unborn babies might need constitutional protection like everyone else. Silence is regrettable regarding either of these mistaken Supreme Court decisions. And I believe it is just as wrong for churches to remain silent as it is for private citizens.

Please understand I'm not suggesting that any church should get involved in partisan politics—Democrats vs. Republicans. That would be a serious mistake. Without entangling itself in political debate, however, our church can and should serve as a moral watchman in the land, speaking out for social justice and civil morality. Our goal is not to enforce but to inform, not to control but to offer counsel. In this advisory role it is entirely appropriate for Adventists to urge the state to preserve liberty and justice for all. Including the unborn.

Some who disagree with me suggest that if abortion has any connection with *religious* concern, then it should not be a matter of *civil* legislation. Well, sexual violence is also a profoundly religious matter, being a violation of the Ten Commandments, but does that remove it from the realm of civil law? Many sins have both religious and civil implications. The question for legislators and the courts to grapple with is whether a particular law can stand on its own without being supported by religious belief.

Even though one's primary motive in avoiding such sins as rape and murder might well be religious, those crimes can be prohibited solely on secular grounds without any reference to religion. But no such civil justification exists to enforce such purely religious matters as school prayer or Sunday keeping.

What about legislation to forbid birth control? The Roman Catholic Church has its own theology of sex that condemns birth control of any kind as sinful (although surveys show that many American Catholics reject Rome's position). The discussion is an internal church matter outside the realm of civil law. Birth control doesn't threaten human life as does abortion. Therefore, the debate about birth control should be restricted to the realm of religious morality, while abortion extends to the public arena of civil morality.

The key question concerning abortion legislation is whether the fetus is a living person, since the state has a civil responsibility to protect human life and property. If abortion didn't stop a beating heart, it would be merely a religious matter like birth control. But since an unborn baby is alive, it deserves the same protection afforded by the Constitution to all people.

We must remind ourselves again and again that religious beliefs concerning abortion are not the issue here. Only because anti-abortion legislation preserves human life does it fall within the realm of civil morality.

Pornography

Another area of dispute regarding civil morality is the restriction of pornography. Many who personally despise it still defend its existence, in order to safeguard their own constitutional right of free speech. They wish to avoid censorship at all costs. In reality, however, don't all of us believe in censorship to some degree? What responsible citizen would defend child pornography, the criminal exploitation of children? Obviously certain boundaries must be set—unlimited free expression cannot exist.

The key question regarding pornography is: Where do we draw the line? Well, what did our founding fathers have in mind when they guaranteed free speech in the First Amendment? Students of history know that Jefferson, Madison, and Washington were guarding against religious and political repression. Do you think they would have risked their lives so that bloodthirsty audiences could be inspired by psycho killer thrillers? How long can society retain its sanity while tolerating the shocking, revolting abuse of women? Must we put up with a volcano of violence and smut to protect the First Amendment?

Greedy pornographers are quick to remind us about their First Amendment rights. But don't women and children have rights as well? Don't they have the right to walk our streets without fear of attack?

Some say, "If you don't like pornography, just stay away from it. Don't buy it, don't look at it, ignore it." They miss the point. Others are buying, others are consuming pornography— molesters, rapists, and murderers. According to an FBI study of serial murderers, the common interest they share most is an obsession with pornography. Evidently, when those who tend toward violence view the violence in hard-core pornography, they hear an evil voice whispering, "Go and do thou likewise."

Figure it out for yourself. If pornography induces only a tenth of one percent of American men to assault women and children, nearly 10,000 rapists, molesters, and murderers would be unleashed.

Some will concede at this point that violent pornography is bad, but simple nudity is OK. Not really. According to the testimony of criminals themselves, so-called soft-core pornography such as *Playboy* magazine opens the door to hard-core, violent pornography. Many believe it also contributes to our staggering divorce rate. Think about how many men are abandoning their wives for younger women. Can one possible reason be that pornography has spoiled their appreciation for what they already had at home? Divorce cases clog our already overstuffed court system.

Beyond that, boys without Dad around are far more prone to join gangs and become criminals. Pornographers must accept some of the blame for America's shattered families. I believe we can and we must oppose pornography because it threatens the public good. Not on the basis of religious preference, of course, since faith cannot be legislated.

Nineteenth-century precedent

Some Adventists who resist the legislation of civil morality forget that our church has never been shy about promoting ordinances that regulate liquor licenses and public smoking. In fact, our pioneers left us a distinguished heritage of campaigning for civil morality that few of us realize or appreciate. But what happens when a legitimate campaign for civil morality gets entangled with a mistaken push for religious legislation?

A crisis of this nature developed in the late nineteenth century when the alcohol prohibition movement linked forces with the drive for a national Sunday law. Seventh-day Adventist leaders at their General Conference session debated what to do. The *Minneapolis Tribune* reported on the discussion in an article entitled, "The Sunday Question." "First and foremost was the question of Prohibition and the keeping of the Sabbath [Sunday], for the proper observance of which the W.C.T.U. [Women's Christian Temperance Union] is now making such strenuous exertions."[1]

Notice the decision of the church council: "Resolved, That while we pledge ourselves to labor earnestly and zealously for the prohibition of the liquor traffic, we hereby utter an earnest protest against connecting with the temperance movement any legislation which discriminates in favor of any religious class or institution, or which tends to the infringement of anybody's religious liberty, and that we cannot sustain or encourage any temperance party or any other organization which indorses [sic] or favors such legislation."[2]

Wise words here. Church leaders did promote legislation requiring government enforcement of civil morality (prohibition), but not religious morality (Sunday keeping). They opposed legislation that "discriminates in favor of any religious class or institution, or which tends to the infringement of anybody's religious liberty." In other words, civil legislation—yes; religious legislation—no.

Some Christians concerned about religious liberty defend the practice of abortion. They fear that the same moral crusaders now fighting the cause of pro-life will eventually cross the line from civil morality into a campaign for religious morality. No doubt millions who seek to outlaw abortion might campaign with equal zeal to restrict religious liberty, but should that keep us from upholding necessary civil morality—protecting law and order, life and property (including unborn life)?

I think not. If our purpose for opposing abortion legislation is simply to preserve our own life and liberty, that would be sad indeed. It would mean that we care more about saving ourselves than saving innocent unborn babies. Such cowardly selfishness seems quite the opposite of what Jesus taught about laying down our lives for our brethren. Our Lord also said, "Inasmuch as you did it to one of the least of these My brethren, you did it to Me" (Matthew 25:40).

We might learn something from the example of Ellen White, who was a fervent crusader for civil morality. She campaigned vigorously for legislation supporting prohibition, joining forces with the WCTU. Even after that organization jumped on the Sunday law bandwagon, she maintained her public association with it. The *Minneapolis Journal* (October 20, 1888) reported: "All her life she has been prominent in temperance work and next Sunday she will address the W.C.T.U."[3]

A remarkable incident indeed. Ellen White, a fervent Sabbath keeper, became an honored guest of the very ones who pushed so hard for a national Sunday law! She somehow managed to keep from compromising her convictions. No doubt her speech to the WCTU, while commending its eagerness for civil morality, also expressed cautions about its encroachment in the area of religious morality.

So Ellen White refused to cross the sacred line between civil and religious morality yet took an active stand with the James Dobsons of her day. Instead of opposing those who promote civil morality, we would do well to heed her counsel:

> We need at this time to show a decided interest in the work of the Woman's Christian Temperance Union. . . . It would be a good thing if at our camp meetings we should invite the members of the W. C. T. U. to take part in our exercises. This would help them to become acquainted with the reasons of our faith, and open the way for us to unite

with them in the temperance work. . . . *In some matters, the workers of the W. C. T. U. are far in advance of our leaders.* . . . I have been surprised as I have seen the indifference of some of our leaders to this organization.[4]

Strange bedfellows

No doubt if Ellen White were alive today, she would find little common cause with groups like People for the American Way. Founded by Hollywood magnate Norman Lear, PAW resists all attempts to "impose" morality on the entertainment business. Lear's group is the moral equivalent of the Tobacco Institute. Both organizations bask in the glorious freedoms afforded by the First Amendment: "This is America! We have freedom! You can't tell us not to advertise tobacco. You can't tell us not to publish pornography."

We must wonder whether the real motive transcends patriotism. Are Lear and those who travel with him possibly trying to protect their multibillion-dollar sin businesses? What do Christians have in common with merchants of vice? In this connection, the texts come to mind, "What communion has light with darkness?" "Come out from among them and be separate" (2 Corinthians 6:14, 17).

Back in Old Testament times, God's people tried to safeguard themselves from the nation of Babylon by forming ties with its mortal foe, godless Egypt. Their plan backfired, however, merely inciting Babylon to come and invade Jerusalem.

In our time, what will happen when an abortion-desensitized society determines that certain Christians are not viable citizens? The decision will be made to abort them with a death decree. Impossible, we may imagine, but this is precisely the prophetic scenario predicted in Revelation chapter 13. Christians who promote abortion to save themselves will someday face a backlash from a society reacting against immorality. *Backlash*—a word to keep in mind when we are tempted to cast our lot with those who oppose morality.

Shouldn't we follow Ellen White's example and support fellow Christians in their battle against immorality? We are making a terrible mistake if we don't.

Many evangelical Christians are frustrated with those who profess to honor God's law while refusing to join them in upholding the sixth commandment. They are distressed to see churches welcome as members in good standing those who spend the working days of the week aborting babies—as long as they stop the killing long enough to honor the Lord's Day.

Whether people honor the Bible Sabbath is not a matter of civil morality. Abortion is, however, since it is a threat to human life. In my opinion, it therefore should be made illegal.

Saving lives?

You may be worrying that outlawing abortion will return us to the old days of illegal abortions with coat hangers, resulting in many infections and deaths. How many would actually die if abortion again became illegal? *Time* magazine reports that in 1972, the year before *Roe vs. Wade*, eleven women lost their lives through illegal abortions. That's tragic. Keep in mind, though, that even legalized abortions are already an act of death.

Parallel to this argument for legalizing abortion is the one for legalizing narcotics use. Those in favor argue that because of the laws making it illegal to use or sell drugs, heroin and cocaine addicts must presently go underground, thus making themselves vulnerable to crime and disease. Legalizing narcotics will diminish the disease factor, they assert. Perhaps, but consider what our society would become. In your local shopping mall, next door to the Pro-choice Abortion Clinic, you would see Drugs R Us— offering discounts for frequent fliers on marijuana highs.

If narcotics were legalized, illegal drug deals would diminish, but the basic problem of addiction itself would escalate. And this is exactly what has happened because of legalizing abortion. "Pregnancy terminations" have skyrocketed, and we are losing a million and a half babies a year!

Some see no problem with that loss of humanity. They suggest that aborted babies are unwanted babies, so society can do without them. Such reasoning is regrettable, when you think about the value of human life. Besides, are aborted babies truly unwanted? Childless couples who want to adopt must often wait for years because of the shortage of babies due to abortion.

Compassion, not condemnation

Should women who get abortions be punished by society? No, they need compassion, not condemnation. Most pro-life activists I know recognize this. One of the most unfair tactics of militant abortionists is to categorize pro-lifers as stern-faced legalists who would love to bomb every abortion clinic in the country, perhaps even bombing people who are getting abortions inside the clinics.

When was the last time you heard of pro-lifers trying to kill mothers who seek abortion? A minority of those who wish to reverse *Roe vs. Wade* do go to extremes by harassing woman who are getting abortions. That should not be, even when the goal is to promote laws that will save human life. However, I have found that the great majority of pro-lifers are concerned, gentle Christians who care deeply about unwed mothers as well as their babies. Likewise, most Christians I know who favor abortion rights are also compassionate and dedicated. If only they realized that a human life has been sacrificed every time a woman leaves the abortion clinic—pregnant no longer.

But logically, wouldn't those who favor pro-life legislation condemn mothers who have opted for abortion as murderers? No. *Murder* is not the word for a confused woman seeking to cope with a major life crisis. A better term for her distressed action would be manslaughter under mitigating circumstances. However, those who reap profits from running illegal abortion clinics would be suitable targets of criminal prosecution. The poor mother is more a victim than a villain.

The real loser

As it stands now, the real loser is the aborted baby. Abortion may be the ultimate child abuse. And unless we take some kind of action to stop the killing, it will get worse. French scientists are promoting a pill that induces abortion without even seeing a doctor. Chemical warfare against the unborn, some would say.

Even if we disregard the couples who would be happy to adopt a baby and suppose that most aborted babies are truly unwanted by anyone—does that mean they are not entitled to protection under the law? Millions are suffering in this world, but only a small percentage opt for suicide. Evidently life, miserable though it may be, seems preferable to death. At least, believing as we do in freedom of choice, should we not let babies grow up and then decide for themselves whether they want to live or die?

If abortion were abolished, many mothers at first would be extremely unhappy about having to bear their babies. Pregnancy often involves tremendous financial hardship and inconvenience. But once a baby is born, few mothers would exchange their darling little intruder for all the money in the world. Their "accident" turns out to be a tremendous blessing. I believe many would-be abortive mothers would change their minds and be thankful that society had required them to preserve the life of their little ones.

When all is said and done, the debate about abortion legislation comes down to the beating heart of an unborn baby and whether that human life shares the constitutional right to life, liberty, and the pursuit of happiness enjoyed by everyone else. Although abortion does have significance for believers because it tampers with life from God, Christian conviction cannot be the basis of pro-life legislation. Religious preference is emphatically not the issue here. Protecting human life is a basic principle of civil morality.

Freedom of choice

And what about freedom of choice as guaranteed by the Bill of Rights? Remember, if a woman willingly engages in sexual intercourse and becomes pregnant, then she has already exercised her free choice. Now it's time to protect the baby's right to choose its own future. Apparently the only way to be consistently pro-choice is to become an abolitionist regarding abortion.

Is saving our babies' lives worth all the turmoil involved in campaigning for civil legislation? Some timid believers in Germany knew something about the atrocities of Hitler's government, yet they kept quiet as millions perished. Now, amid the present abortion holocaust in America, may God help us to be different. May He strengthen us to stand up and be counted for our moral convictions.

In summary, civil laws such as the abolition of abortion and the restriction of pornography are needed for preserving life and property. Laws designed to enforce religious preference, however, are a dangerous threat to freedom of conscience. We must learn to distinguish between the moral behavior Caesar requires and that which the conscience owes to God, and God alone.

---

1. Ellen G. White Estate, comp., *Manuscripts and Memories of Minneapolis 1888* (Boise, Idaho: Pacific Press, 1988), 559.

2. Ibid., 560.

3. Ibid., 534.

4. "The Temperance Work," *Review and Herald*, 15 October 1914. She also said: "Some of our best talent should be set at work for the W. C. T. U., not as antagonists but as those who fully appreciate the good that has been done by this body. We should seek to gain the confidence of the workers in the W. C. T. U. by harmonizing with them as far as possible. We are to let them see and understand that the foundation of the principles of our doctrine is the Word of God" ("Cooperation With the WCTU and Other Temperance Organizations," *Manuscript Releases*, vol. 1., 124).

In support of someone who had been criticized by radical separationists in our church, Ellen White wrote: "I thank the Lord with heart, and soul, and voice that you have been a prominent and influential member of the Women's Christian Temperance Union" (ibid., 125.)

Chapter 6

The Betrayal of Women

(Feminism)

On a sunny afternoon in May 1976, the week before my son was born, I was picking up mail at the post office. The clerk, a fervent feminist, never missed an opportunity to cheerfully admonish male customers about cross-gender responsibilities. After congratulating me on the upcoming blessed event, she launched into another sermon, concluding: "Remember now, don't be one of those husbands who lets his wife get up at night to feed the baby!"

"I'm happy to do everything possible to help Darlene," I assured her. Trying to suppress a grin, I added: "But if the Lord intends for me to nurse the baby, He neglected to give me the needed equipment." With a triumphant wave I was out the door, glad for the opportunity to contribute something to the ongoing debate about feminism.

I do believe in a form of feminism, after the New Testament model: "There is neither Jew nor Greek, there is neither slave nor free, there is neither male nor female; for you are all one in Christ Jesus" (Galatians 3:28).

So men and women are equal through the gospel—equal in value, but not identical in function. I don't claim to understand all the implications of this, and if you feel I'm mistaken in what you'll read here, please forgive me.

I'll begin by affirming my enthusiasm for a woman's equal

right to become whatever God wants her to be. My wife Darlene's highest ambition has always been to use her talents in the traditional home-based role of wife and mother, although she works as a secretary to help feed our cats and pay the mortgage. Our teenage daughter, Christi, has a different vision for herself; she wants to use her talents in a salaried profession. And why not? Shouldn't any woman be free to fulfill the role God has equipped her to fill, whether in the home, the office, or anywhere else? Even in the church? Especially in the church! It's simply wrong to deny women their God-given calling.

There are differences

This doesn't mean that sex roles are interchangeable except for reproductive functions. Hormonal differences between men and women stimulate profound emotional and behavioral variances. *Time* magazine reports:

> During the feminist revolution of the 1970s, talk of inborn differences in the behavior of men and women was distinctly unfashionable, even taboo. Men dominated fields like architecture and engineering, it was argued, because of social, not hormonal, pressures. Women did the vast majority of society's child rearing because few other options were available to them. Once sexism was abolished, so the argument ran, the world would become a perfectly equitable, androgynous place, aside from a few anatomical details.
>
> But biology has a funny way of confounding expectations. Rather than disappear, the evidence for innate sexual differences only began to mount. . . . Researchers found subtle neurological differences between the sexes both in the brain's structure and in its functioning. In addition, another generation of parents discovered that, despite their best efforts to give baseballs to their daughters and sewing kits to their sons, girls still flocked to dollhouses while boys clambered into tree forts. Perhaps nature is more important than nurture after all.[1]

Recent studies suggest that there may be some real differences after all. And why not? We have different hormones

and body parts; it would be odd if our brains were 100 percent unisex.[2]

Why are men typically more aggressive and violent than
women? Basically because of the male hormone testosterone.
And so men commit most of the murders, rapes, and armed
robberies. Think of the many wars of conquest that could have
been avoided if male leaders had paid heed to the nurturing
instinct of mothers and wives who yearned to keep their sons and
husbands at home. Even in times of peace men have bullied their
way around the world, the nation, and the home. Zealous male
leadership is a blessing, of course, when sanctified by God's grace.

Women, too, have their own unique characteristics and capabilities. Due to their hormonal makeup, they are more likely to
become depressed than men. The other side to that coin is their
tenderness and sensitivity. And women's famous intuition is no
rumor; they are more adept than men at discerning emotions.
"When shown pictures of actors portraying various feelings,
women outscore men in identifying the correct emotion."[3] They
also have a capacity for detail; in one experiment women were
70 percent better at remembering the location of items on a
desktop. Men do better than women at visualizing projects and
perhaps at reading maps.

Verbal differences too

Regarding verbal habits, Dr. Arlene Taylor of St. Helena Hospital and Health Center notes that men

> speak more in public than in private and use approximately
> 12,000 words a day—most of them before they come home to
> their families after work. . . . Girls begin talking earlier
> [than boys] and talk more about everything their whole lives
> (50,000 words a day). Talk is used to establish rapport and
> to create intimacy. Their conversation is filled with people,
> feelings, personal experiences, and health interests.[4]

You've probably observed that women tend to talk about relationships or feelings, whereas men talk more about activities,

such as business projects or sports. To men, being respected is paramount; women want to be appreciated.

Yes, there are differences between men and women, praise the Lord! Of course, some individuals shatter gender stereotypes, like the lady at the circus who sports a better mustache than I'm growing. Generally, though, men are more likely to have visible facial hair than women. Agreed? Women have other endowments, but men are usually taller and stronger. My point is that there are differences—physical, hormonal, and emotional—between men and women and that these differences qualify them for different roles in life. Equally important roles, but different ones.

For the most part—not always—men are explorers, and women are homemakers; men are warriors, and women are unifiers; men create, and women adapt; men build houses, and women decorate them. Men instinctively shelter the women they love, and most women like it that way. I believe that the typical woman wants a man strong enough to lead her and watch over her, as long as he is kind, nonmanipulative, and respectful of her equality. Some women, of course, don't want a man at all. Probably one of them wrote the bumper sticker I saw recently: "The more I know men, the more I love my dog."

Very funny. Very sad.

The feminist betrayal

I blame men much more than women for the misunderstanding between the sexes; we are the ones who invented the inequities. However, radical feminists overreact when they make blanket pronouncements such as: "The best man for the job is a woman." Most women don't buy into their unisex agenda. Consider the 1984 U.S. election, a golden opportunity to install a woman one step away from the Oval Office. Democratic vice-presidential candidate Geraldine Ferraro was an articulate, intelligent politician with impeccable feminist credentials who promised to fight for women's rights. And yet the women of America declined the golden opportunity she offered to "liberate" themselves from total male leadership.

Feminist leaders themselves often take secret vacations from their militant mind-set, as documented in a *Reader's Digest* article by Sally Quinn, "The Feminist Betrayal." She observes:

Feminists have made some amazing revelations lately. Gloria Steinem, in her new book, admits to seducing a man by playing down the person she was and playing up the person he wanted her to be. . . . Jane Fonda, talking to *Time* about her new husband, Ted Turner, announces that she's given up acting for now. "Ted is not a man you leave to go on location," she explains. "He needs you there all the time."

Barbara Streisand, in a Washington *Post* interview, says that "even though my feminist side says people should be independent and not need to be taken care of by another person, it doesn't necessarily work that way."[5]

Quinn asks, "What are we to make of all this? Is it possible that feminism as we have known it is dead? I think so. Like communism in the former Soviet empire, the movement in its present form has outlasted its usefulness."[6]

Of course, feminist leaders would deny that assessment, along with a further charge from this well-respected female author:

The people who spoke for the feminist movement were never completely honest with women. They were hypocritical. And like the communists who denied the existence of God and the right to worship, leaders of the feminist movement overlooked the deepest, most fundamental needs of their constituency. . . . Instead of helping women fulfill their needs, helping the "total woman," they acted as if women had but one side and ignored the reality of husbands and children. *You can do it all, look at us*, was the message. Women who struggled to make it work and failed were often hurt more than helped by these phony examples of how wonderful life could be if only they would take charge and discard the men. Women felt ashamed to be housewives, ashamed to be full-time mothers.

By trivializing the important issues in people's personal lives, dismissing what really goes on in the hearts and minds of women, the movement hurt itself and offered a target for its enemies. . . . The truth is, many women have come to see the feminist movement as anti-male, anti-child, anti-family and anti-feminine. And therefore it has nothing to do with us.[7]

Sexual outrage

All that may be true, but you don't have to be Einstein to understand what makes many feminists bitter about men. It's the way they often abuse their power. The worst of them kill, rape, or harass, and many of the best are insensitive to feminine feelings. Considering the terrible treatment women have suffered from men since time began, the wonder is not why so many have hatred and bitterness but why there isn't more of it!

Perhaps the greatest injustice men bring upon women is abusing them sexually, then letting them bear the blame. If sex happens on a date, it's her fault. If pregnancy results, it's her problem. If she gets raped, maybe she was asking for it; at least she might have prevented it by dressing differently or staying home after dark. No wonder most rapes go unreported; women don't want their private lives dragged out into the public record through a courtroom circus. A rape victim on the witness stand is at the mercy of her attacker's lawyer with his cunning intimidation, insults, and insinuations. Curious spectators and reporters, with pencils poised, watch the whole show—worst of all the leering attacker himself. Every humiliating aspect of the crime is discussed; even the underwear she wore may be waved in front of the courtroom and examined by the jurists. Her precious privacy is stripped away, laying bare a quivering victim on the altar of community gossip.

In essence a rape victim is assaulted again by the legal system, not in some dark alley but in the public spotlight. Finally, after all is said and done and the jury returns its verdict, too often the original rapist goes free to prowl the streets again, thanks to some legal loophole. This is how the wheels of justice roll over women. No wonder the feminists are angry. I am too, aren't you?

Yes, a man accused of rape is entitled to his day in court. But every effort should be made to preserve the rights of the victim too. Just when society has begun to protect the privacy of a rape victim by limiting the range of questions defense attorneys can ask regarding her background, along comes a new threat from the media. Many reporters are demanding the right to broadcast her name on the six o'clock news, thus exposing her to further scrutiny and suspicion from strangers, neighbors, and coworkers. She becomes a potential victim of harassing phone calls and further violence from those who prey upon the vulnerable.

How sad! How wrong!

But what about the public's "right to know"? That's not as important as a victim's right to heal.

When a woman has been assaulted, society should hunt down her attacker and punish him, meanwhile inflicting a minimum of disruption and embarrassment upon the victim. Otherwise, it might be impossible for her to ever put the nightmare behind her.

Devastated victims

Most men can't comprehend how devastated a woman or girl feels after having sex forced upon her. Long after experiencing rape or incest—perhaps even for the rest of her life—the victim may imagine herself as dirty and worthless. She is often frigid and terrified of repeat attacks. Worst of all, she typically blames herself, as least in part, for being violated.

Males can be victims too. As a boy I was twice the victim of nonviolent sexual offenses: once by the older brother of a friend and again by a strange man at the bus station in Hackensack, New Jersey. Both encounters were obnoxious to me, but I was able to shrug them off and get on with life.

I'm not suggesting that all boys manage to brush aside intrusions upon their sexual privacy. Many experience shame and guilt for years to come. Girls and women, though, seem to have a more complex and delicate emotional makeup that multiplies their suffering. I've concluded that society needs to take drastic measures to protect women from assault. In certain cases of aggravated rape, I think offenders should even be punished with permanent sexual incapacity.

That's right!

And depending upon the degree of offense, adding a prison term might be appropriate. Harsh? Yes, but justified because of the damage a woman suffers when raped—especially in this age of AIDS and incurable venereal diseases.

Unless you or a woman you love has been the victim of violent sexual assault and you have tasted the bitter trauma imposed by our legal system—if they ever catch the assailant—you might dispute my concept of justice. But on one point I think you will agree. With such punishment facing them, potential rapists would likely think twice before committing their first assault. And permanent sexual incapacity would tend to eliminate repeat offenses, don't you think?

What about rehabilitation? I'm all for that. Let convicted rapists learn to live as peaceful citizens—without their means of sexual violence! No doubt some would become even more dangerous as a result. So lock them up for life. If they kill someone, remember what the Bible says: "Whoever sheds man's blood, by man his blood shall be shed" (Genesis 9:6).

Well, that's how I see it. You may not agree. I predicted you wouldn't agree with everything you read in this book—and that's all right.

Severe punishment of sexual violence against women is one goal of feminists with which I fully concur. Whatever the cost to the criminal, society must protect its vulnerable citizens.

Beloved criminals

Much of the crime against women takes place in the home, from the men they want to love. Incest and spousal abuse are far more common than imagined, even in churchgoing families. Men often regard their wives and daughters as property, to treat any way they wish. Nothing could be farther from God's plan for the home.

If any type of abuse is happening to you or to someone you know, get help quickly. Don't allow yourself to be abused even verbally. Adapt to your situation Paul's counsel to vulnerable Timothy: "Let no one despise your youth, but be an example to the believers in word, in conduct, in love, in spirit, in faith, in purity" (1 Timothy 4:12). For you this means not letting any man despise or ridicule your womanhood. Let the offender know that as a daughter of heaven's King, you deserve better treatment from him. I'm not suggesting starting a shouting match or trading insults. Such conduct is unbecoming a Christian. Just a few well-chosen, well-spoken words can kindle respect for you.

Last week I attended a meeting with Nancy Canwell, an associate pastor of the college church in College Place, Washington. She was answering a question when a man thoughtlessly interrupted her and began voicing his own views. Nancy didn't get upset, but neither did she ignore the intrusion upon her ministry. Immediately she turned, looked at him, and softly said: "Excuse me." She then continued speaking where he had cut her off. Nobody interrupted her the rest of the day!

Nancy is firm yet polite, calmly assertive without seeming aggressive. She is such a pleasant person that she doesn't come across as pushy—but neither does she want to get pushed around. Men often need reminders that women are fellow human beings with equal access rights to the sound waves inside classrooms, boardrooms, and dining rooms. Women deserve commendation for showing this to America and to the world.

Points of agreement

We can also appreciate the contribution feminists have made with the concept of equal pay for equal work. Although society has made progress, women in general still receive lower wages than male counterparts comparably employed—only about sixty cents on the dollar compared to men. Such injustice severely penalizes women.

Even after women retire, American society denies them equality. Consider how we tax widows. Fewer than 5 percent of all widows fifty-five years old or older ever remarry. And while widows in the United States pay heavy inheritance taxes, widowers pay none at all. The average income of widows is below that of their male counterparts, yet they are the ones penalized by tax laws. Is this equality?

One of the many subtle ways society discriminates against women is in the architecture of buildings, public and private— even churches. You've noticed the long lines outside women's restrooms between innings at ballgames and between services at church. After suffering an unjustified inconvenience, a woman emerges to be scolded by her man: "Where have you been all this time!" The real question is, Where has society been all this time?

Well, those are just a few instances of how a male-dominated culture cheats women of basic human dignity. At business meetings where their perceptive insights are needed, women are frequently ignored—only to receive unwanted attention afterward when their male colleagues want to buy them drinks, plying them for sex. Automobile salesmen call women in business suits "Honey" and subject them to a patronizing explanation of the difference between an air bag and air conditioning. Women attorneys, despite thorough preparation, find it difficult to be taken seriously by either judges or peers. Likewise with women in all professions, perhaps to a lesser extent in the realm of education. Female nurses often have problems with male physicians who bark orders with less than the respect that a fellow professional deserves, yet who demand professional performance.

One sad situation I've seen is where the wife of a medical resident worked hard to boost him through those long years of internship and residency, anticipating the rewards that would be theirs after he finally launched his practice. Then, as he hung up his new diploma, he hung her out to dry. Just that quick. A cute young blonde now tools around town in a new red Mercedes that another woman earned with sweat and tears.

Some states have laws protecting women against being robbed this way from potential income; others make no such provision. Such legislation is important, even though no law can heal a broken heart. Think of the millions of women put out to pasture by male teenagers in their forties who pick up women half their age. As Woody Allen testified after acknowledging without apology an affair with his ex-wife's adopted daughter: "There's no logic to it. The heart wants what it wants."

So it does. And what of the scorned wife's shattered heart? Well, she doesn't matter anymore. And she may never manage to attract the fickle eyes of another man, having lost her youthful figure after bearing three babies. Actually, she wouldn't have time for the dating scene anyway—her babies are now teenagers that she must guide alone through the drug-infested rapids of the high-school years. Her only relief comes on those sporadic weekends of loneliness when Disneyland Dad whisks her teenagers away to pay his penance for going AWOL.

Life just doesn't seem fair to the fairer sex. Men don't lose their sexuality when they gain twenty-five pounds and their hair whitens. But then, the Lord never intended for a faithful wife to be forced into a beauty contest with a twenty-two-year-old rival. The resulting epidemic of divorce is a tragedy.

The list of grievances against men could go on and on. Suffice it to say that feminists are well-justified in denouncing the problems women suffer these days. Unfortunately, their solutions are inadequate at best and outrageous at worst.

Reverse chauvinism

As an example of the extremes some feminists feel are justified, consider what happened when the trustees of all-female Mills College in California announced they would allow men to enroll. The students wanted the college to be a sanctuary from men. Perhaps they were afraid men would dominate class discussions. A legitimate concern, perhaps, but the fact is that the human race includes both men and women, and we must learn to do business with each other. Gender-exclusive schools don't facilitate this.

Nevertheless, the women of Mills College seized control of the campus. Many shaved their heads, taped their mouths, and barricaded themselves in front of the ad building. After two weeks of such protests, the trustees relented and reversed their decision. College president Mary Metz proclaimed to the victorious protestors: "Our passion for women's education has made history!" They flung her flattery back in her face. "Not *his*tory!" they shouted indignantly. "We made *her*story!"

Some people must feel an emotional need to be unreasonable. Getting through to them takes the patience and wisdom of Barbara Bush. Remember the fury that erupted in the summer of 1990 on the campus of Wellesley College in Massachusetts when the then–First Lady was invited to speak at the graduation ceremony? A quarter of the senior class reacted in protest.

Why?

"To honor Barbara Bush as a commencement speaker is to honor a woman who has gained recognition through the achievements of her husband, which contradicts what we have been taught over the past four years."

Pity Mrs. Bush for her personal choice of finding satisfaction in standing behind her man! Well, the young radicals at Wellesley found little sympathy from the majority of American women for treating the First Lady like an old fossil. Columnist Erma Bombeck told them: "Sit down. You're not ready to graduate yet. You've got a lot to learn."

Barbara Bush graciously overlooked the insult. She honored Wellesley College with her presence, and with humility and humor explained and personified the nobility of a woman who unselfishly chooses to support her husband and family.

Feminists everywhere might profit from her example.

------

1. Christine Gorman, "Sizing Up the Sexes," *Time*, 20 January 1992, 42.

2. Barbara Ehrenreich, "Making Sense of la Différence," *Time*, 20 January 1992, 51.

3. Gorman, 44.

4. "The Power of Words," *Adventist Review*, 2 April 1992, 24.

5. Sally Quinn, "The Feminist Betrayal," *Reader's Digest*, June 1992, 84.

6. Ibid.

7. Ibid., 84-86.

Chapter 7

Ordination or Submission—or Both?

(Role of women in the church and home)

What is the proper role for women in the church? "Liberals" want to ordain them for ministry, while "conservatives" demand their submission to male leadership. As the debate intensifies, both sides cite support in Scripture. It can get confusing.

What really is God's will for the Christian woman of the nineties?

Long ago the Bible showcased a model of womanhood that sets the stage for us to wrestle with reality in this chapter. We find it in the wisdom of the Proverbs: "Who can find a virtuous wife? For her worth is far above rubies. The heart of her husband safely trusts her; so he will have no lack of gain. She does him good and not evil all the days of her life" (Proverbs 31:10-12).

First, this model wife is faithful to her husband as a "helper suitable" to him, just like Eve, the original wife (see Genesis 2:18, NIV). This doesn't mean she was homebound, baking cookies all day: "She seeks wool and flax, and willingly works with her hands. She is like the merchant ships, she brings her food from afar. . . . She considers a field and buys it; from her profits she plants a vineyard" (Proverbs 31:13-16).

Along with pursuing business on behalf of the family, this model wife also has a social conscience: "She extends her hand to the poor, yes, she reaches out her hands to the needy" (verse 20). Though active in the community, her life centers in her home:

"She also rises while it is yet night, and provides food for her household, and a portion for her maidservants" (verse 15). She is a respected source of counsel, yet it's her husband who represents the family as its elder and leader: "She opens her mouth with wisdom, and on her tongue is the law of kindness." "Her husband is known in the gates, when he sits among the elders of the land" (verses 26, 23).

When all is said and done, this woman finds her family-centered life immensely rewarding: "Her children rise up and call her blessed; her husband also, and he praises her" (verse 28).

Christian wives today, and husbands too, could benefit from studying Proverbs 31 to learn the scriptural pattern for marriage. The woman there doesn't compete with her husband—but neither is she a passive doormat. She and her husband obviously share a close, trusting relationship. Under the umbrella of his leadership, she exerts considerable influence at home and in the community, fully exercising her many talents.

Submission is for everyone

With the pattern of Proverbs 31 in mind, let's look at the Bible's most famous passage about husbands and wives. Ephesians chapter 5 is often abused by men, resented by women, and misunderstood by all:

> Wives, submit to your own husbands, as to the Lord. For the husband is head of the wife, as also Christ is head of the church; and He is the Savior of the body. Therefore, just as the church is subject to Christ, so let the wives be to their own husbands in everything. Husbands, love your wives, just as Christ also loved the church and gave Himself for it (verses 22-25).

Shall we sweep aside our preconceptions and discover what submission really means, according to the Bible?

First, all of us must learn to submit: "Submit to one another out of reverence for Christ" (Ephesians 5:21, NIV). This doesn't mean we all have the same role in life or that there's no such thing as leadership. There are civil leaders we must obey: "Submit yourselves to every ordinance of man for the Lord's sake, whether to the king as supreme, or to governors, as to those who are sent by him for the punishment of evildoers and for the praise of those who do good" (1 Peter 2:13, 14). The Bible also instructs us all, men and women both, to submit to spiritual leaders: "Obey those who rule over you, and be submissive, for they watch out for your souls, as those who must give account" (Hebrews 13:17). This is unpopular instruction indeed, in our age of assertive individuality and congregationalism.

However, leaders have strict limits on their authority. Never give them a blank check signed by your conscience to do whatever they please. The Bible says leaders themselves are accountable to God, who requires them to be unselfish servants of the people. Jesus told His disciples: "You know that those who are considered rulers over the Gentiles lord it over them, and their great ones exercise authority over them. Yet it shall not be so among you; but whoever desires to become great among you shall be your servant. And whoever of you desires to be first shall be slave of all" (Mark 10:42-44).

Christ Himself set the example of servant leadership: "Even the Son of Man did not come to be served, but to serve, and to give His life a ransom for many" (Mark 10:45). Jesus, King of glory, came here to be of service to unworthy humanity. In dying on the cross, He fulfilled the plan of His Father, whom He had obeyed all His life on earth.

The Holy Spirit is unselfish too, not calling attention to Himself but humbly glorifying Jesus as Saviour (see John 16:13, 14). The Father Himself, as the ultimate leader of the universe, tenderly serves the needs of His creation, bestowing sunshine and rain even on unthankful and wicked people.

All heaven is encircled by a spirit of service. The members of the Godhead are unselfish with each other. Angels, in turn, submit to the Father, Son, and Holy Spirit, who delight in meeting their needs as well. Everything was wonderful from eternity onward until Lucifer invented the concept that leadership meant self-exaltation. That's the spirit of this fallen world, where those with power lord it over anyone under their leadership.

Unfortunately, that's the spirit of many husbands toward

their wives. God intended for the husband to be the defender and protector of his wife: "Husbands, love your wives, just as Christ also loved the church and gave Himself for it. . . . So husbands ought to love their own wives as their own bodies; he who loves his wife loves himself" (Ephesians 5:25-28). So just as Christ was the servant leader of the church, so God calls husbands to serve their wives by offering unselfish leadership. Wives, in turn, fulfill their God-appointed role by submitting to their husbands: "Just as the church is subject to Christ, so let the wives be to their own husbands in everything" (Ephesians 5:24). In everything, of course, that does not violate her conscience.

Is submission demeaning?

Is it demeaning for a wife to accept her husband's leadership? Not when the husband considers himself her servant in guiding her, treating her respectfully as his equal. I enjoy my job at the General Conference working for *Ministry* magazine as an associate editor, even though I don't make final decisions. That's the responsibility of executive editor, David Newman. I have a vital role, but I don't make the big decisions. David considers me a partner and consults me when possible. He tries to reach a consensus with his two associate editors, but whenever we can't agree, it's his responsibility to take charge. We trust him to make the best decision, knowing he bears the responsibility for it.

At home, my wife's role is not unlike mine at *Ministry*. She's my associate, my partner. Darlene and I are close enough that I'm always aware of her convictions. I've learned to value her counsel and unique insights, and I do my best to achieve consensus with her. But if we cannot agree and a decision must be made, we both know that the Lord hasn't left the matter up in the air. He says it's the husband's responsibility to do what is best for the family. And I also take the blame if I'm wrong.

Many times a man is far less talented than his wife, but he can still serve as her leader. Often in business and government the chief executive isn't nearly as knowledgeable or capable in many areas as his associates. And if his I.Q. is above room temperature, he will be wise enough to respect their wisdom and abilities. Likewise with husbands and wives. If a man is too ignorant or stubborn to treat a woman as his partner, I wouldn't recommend that she marry him.

So, women, choose your husbands carefully. A growing number of Adventist women remain single, by choice or by circumstance. They have discovered that they don't really need a man to be a whole person. It might be nice if the right one comes along, but until then they are single. In God's plan, however, women who do exercise their option to get married accept their husband's leadership.

Some couples reject God's plan for the family by trying to get along without a leader. They insist that everything run on consensus. Well, fifty/fifty is an ideal to strive for, but the fact is that consensus is sometimes impossible to reach when a decision must be made. Somebody's got to lead, and the husband needs to take charge. If he doesn't, then his wife is automatically in control. There's no such thing as no leadership.

Every ship needs a captain; every office needs a manager; every publication needs a senior editor. And, according to God's plan, every home needs a husband. There must be no arrogance or selfishness on the part of the man and no power struggle on the part of the woman. He serves as her loving and respectful leader; she serves as a helper suitable to him.

No, she doesn't blindly obey her husband without a mind or conscience of her own. Remember, New Testament submission doesn't make the wife a doormat, a second-rate family member, or the property of her husband: "The wife does not have authority over her own body, but the husband does. And likewise the husband does not have authority over his own body, but the wife does" (1 Corinthians 7:4). In other words, the wife should be able to expect as much from her husband as he can from her. Never should she merge her self-identity in his personality.

Ellen White counseled: "Woman should fill the position which God originally designed for her, as her husband's equal. . . . Her individuality cannot be merged in his. She should feel that she is her husband's equal—to stand by his side, she faithful at her post of duty and he at his."[1] While recognizing a woman's equality, Ellen White concurred with the Bible that "the Lord has constituted the husband the head of the wife to be her protector [as Christ gave Himself for the church]."[2]

When you compile what the Bible says about the relationship of husbands and wives, a clear picture emerges: The man must serve his wife and their children by guarding and guiding them, while she assists him with her talents and respect for his leadership. Much is at stake: "Husbands, in the same way be considerate as you live with your wives, and treat them with respect as the weaker partner and as heirs with you of the gracious gift of life, *so that nothing will hinder your prayers*" (1 Peter 3:7, NIV, emphasis supplied).

Lesson from Katie

NBC's Katie Couric is an excellent example of how a richly talented woman can find fulfillment under the umbrella of strong male leadership. Notice how she describes her relationship with co-host and longtime fixture Bryant Gumbel on the "Today" show:

> Yes, he can be intimidating, if you let him be. If he senses weakness, I think he sort of chews you up and spits you out. . . . The way to get along with Bryant is do your homework, don't let him drown and he won't let you drown. He's still the captain of the ship in terms of guiding it. But I do feel like an equal partner with him in terms of the division of labor. . . . I've been in television journalism for eleven years and I didn't want to be this sidekick who sort of giggled and did the features."[3]

Many media experts believe that newcomer Katie Couric is already more valuable to the telecast than Gumbel. Yet, she doesn't see herself in competition with him—nor is she a doormat. Gumbel respects her talents, and she finds satisfaction using them to complement his gifts. In doing so she has singlehandedly resurrected a show that had plunged in the ratings. Her producer testifies, "Katie has buoyed a lot of people. . . . She's a breath of fresh air."

Morning by morning, Katie Couric shows America how women can make a compelling contribution in a support role. Many women truly enjoy working under the umbrella of male leadership—they are by nature more cooperative and less forceful than men are. Dr. Arlene Taylor observed that "female speech contains more qualifiers ('maybe,' 'perhaps'). . . [and] is more indirect. Proposals for actions are *suggested* by 'How about . . .?' or 'Why don't we . . .?' "[4]

Most feminists insist that a woman's tendency to try to please people is unnatural and culturally conditioned. They try to project toughness, but it doesn't work. Just having a high-pitched voice sets a woman leader at a disadvantage. A deep-voiced man can often command respect by projecting his voice, but a woman who tries that is usually perceived as shrill and out of control. Whether or not this reflects cultural conditioning, whether or not it is fair, it is reality.

Two traps

Women who function as senior leaders often fall into one of two traps. They may compensate for their disadvantages with a tough, bossy style. Men can often get away with this, but women seldom can.

At the other extreme, many women find themselves uncomfortable and unwilling to exercise their authority. Frequently the problem is not with her but with her constituency; every leader needs cooperative followers. And the fact is that most people— women as well as men—are unprepared to pledge allegiance to a woman chief. Whether we like it or not, that's the way it is, at least for now.

On the world scene, two women presidents, elected to succeed male dictators, struggled to assert themselves against the leftover establishment. Corazon Aquino of the Philippines and Violeta Chamorro of Nicaragua impressed voters that they could lead with integrity, fairness, and compassion. Unfortunately, sincere intentions weren't enough to make them successful leaders. Aquino eventually found herself spurned by her electorate, and Chamorro is currently struggling for political survival against the entrenched power of the Sandinista regime.

The mayor of Washington, D.C., Sharon Pratt Kelly, likewise attracted voters with her pledge to clean up crime in the nation's capital. Despite good intentions, Kelly also is struggling to exert leadership. If she were a man, she might have an easier time asserting authority. Too many women who could flourish in a support role fail to deliver the hard-driving leadership necessary to overcome the ever-present opposition.

There are brilliant exceptions, and we must leave the door open to them. Consider Margaret Thatcher, former prime minister of Great Britain. Many believe the "iron lady" was the finest world leader of the last decade. Among Adventists, some members believe that the most effective academic administrator in North America is Loma Linda's Lyn Behrens. Such women as Behrens and Thatcher are specially gifted in commanding respect from men without seeming bossy.

If this world were a better place, women would have an easier time exercising leadership. But in our dog-eat-dog society, women are often cannibalized by chauvinism. Whenever push comes to shove, they find themselves pushed around and stepped upon. Although most women resent such abuse, they find it difficult if not impossible to overcome it. Frustrated at having their hopes and feelings suppressed, many women become walking volcanoes, ready to erupt with rage. This helps explain the feminist movement. Many quietly submissive wives are just as angry in their traditional roles as are the outspoken feminists, but they turn their fury inward, which forces them into a deep and dark cavern of depression.

Male suppression not only fosters female depression; it also hurts society and the church. There is no greater frustration for Christian women than the lack of opportunity to exercise their spiritual gifts. With this in mind, let's examine the ministry of women.

Women in ministry

Based on all we've discussed so far, I hope you agree that women are fully equal with men as workers for Christ—equal but not identical. The work of women is similar to that of the Holy Spirit in the Godhead—an equal partner whose role is not executive but supportive as a helper. In my opinion, being feminine qualifies a woman for a nurturing pastoral role more frequently than serving as a president or senior pastor. Her intuition and sensitivity enable her to perform many pastoral functions better than the average man, particularly as a counselor and as a specialty associate on multiperson staffs. A woman pastor can safely get close to female parishioners, who form the majority of church membership. Many male pastors who became sexually involved with women counselees might have been saved from disaster had they entrusted the case to a female associate.

So we really need women ministers, both as salaried pastors and volunteer local elders. Beyond the pastoral functions already mentioned, their unique insights are valuable in the pulpit. Do you feel uncomfortable with sermons from a woman preacher? Once upon a time I did too. And then it dawned on me: How can I accept the ministry of Ellen White while rejecting other women?

Based on the compelling ministry of our prophet, Adventists, of all people, ought to appreciate the role of women in ministry. Yet many fundamentalist members vigorously protest against women who preach—even while regarding the sermons of Ellen White as having authority equal to Scripture. How bizarre! One woman they practically turn into a female pope, while they automatically reject the ministry of all other women. What sense does this make?

Ellen White didn't find it necessary to request official ordination, but she did carry ministerial credentials—and she had spiritual authority far exceeding any Adventist minister or administrator, then or now. However, our prophet did not seek executive authority in the church; she accepted the leadership of male presidents.

Recently Dr. Arlene Taylor took a worldwide survey of Adventist women who hold the highest positions of responsibility available to them in our church. Even they could not agree that senior executive leadership posts should be staffed by fellow women. Only 49 percent said it would be appropriate for a fellow woman to serve as a local church senior pastor; 46 percent were comfortable with a woman as a mission/conference/union president, and 40 percent as a division/General Conference president.[5]

Keep in mind, though, that some women do function superbly in top leadership. Whenever men are absent, women must press to the front. Millions of mothers serve nobly and ably as the spiritual leaders of their families. In times of crisis, with male leaders in prison or otherwise unable to function, women have taken up the torch and performed as well as men.

There is nothing immoral or unscriptural about such service for Christ. Some would disagree, pointing to texts that enjoin silence upon women in church. The question is whether this was a temporary prohibition because of New Testament culture or an eternal principle, binding women in all times and places. I believe Paul sometimes used theological reasoning to support the requirements of his culture. If I'm mistaken, then we must muzzle women from teaching as well as preaching. And once again, where would that leave us with Ellen White?

It only makes sense for women of the nineties to break the ancient cultural code of silence. That being the case, I know of no Scripture that stands in the way of ordaining them for whatever position the church sees fit to entrust to them. Did you know that the General Conference in session actually voted the ordination of women back in 1881? Unfortunately, the officers neglected to implement this official action of the church body. Now, more than a century later, the time may be ripe to move forward.

I believe the church is slowly moving in that direction. Although delegates at the last General Conference session turned down the ordination of women, they did approve the commissioning of women as ministers, licensed (but not ordained) to perform full pastoral functions within their own districts and elsewhere with special approval. So now in the Seventh-day Adventist Church, local divisions are free to authorize women to teach, preach, baptize, marry, and bury.

Most resistance to actually ordaining women comes from outside the North American Division in places where local leaders have justly complained about Americans enforcing Western customs and practices in their regions. Pushing Western culture on others isn't fair—and the reverse isn't fair, either. I think the NAD, or any other division, should be free to move ahead on its own with the ordination of women, since such a practice would not affect morality or doctrine.

But what about unity in the church—shouldn't we all be doing the same thing regarding women? Not necessarily. Remember that unity isn't uniformity. While Adventists everywhere share the same message and mission, cultural practice varies from place to place. In New Testament times believers received approval to adapt religious custom to local culture (see Acts 15). In harmony with this biblical example, it seems that North America and other fields ought to have self-determination regarding the ordination of their own women. But we must wait until the world church sees fit to give the green light.

Meanwhile, women have plenty of opportunity under the present policy to serve the Lord and His church. Those who aggressively lobby for "higher" positions are probably not equipped emotionally for pastoral work of any kind (nor are men who do this). Hard-nosed tactics offend both men and women. An abrasive attitude makes it difficult to win loyalty and achieve consensus, as every leader must.

If women pastors continue to quietly and faithfully perform their ministries, I believe the church will eventually be compelled to ordain them on the basis of their fruitfulness in ministry. Back in early church history, prejudiced Jewish Christians withheld baptism from Gentile believers. Finally they dropped their resistance—not because the Gentiles picketed the Jerusalem Council, but because of the undeniable evidence of the Holy Spirit's gift to them. Peter argued before the General Conference of his day, " 'If God gave them the same gift as he gave us, . . . who was I to think that I could oppose God?' When they heard this, they had no further objections and praised God" (Acts 11:17, 18, NIV).

I believe that someday we will be compelled to exclaim, "How can we withhold ordination from those whom God has so evidently gifted and blessed?"

Christ's will for women

Let me sum up our discussion of the last two chapters by asking the question, Was Jesus a feminist? That depends how we define the term. If we understand it to mean having respect for women as being of equal importance with men through creation and redemption, then, yes, Jesus was a type of feminist. He encouraged and valued their devoted service to His kingdom. But nothing in His Word sanctions the radical agenda of some modern feminists, who deny the dignity and reality of Christian submission in marriage and the fact that men are generally better suited to function as senior leaders in the church and in society. (Of course, as I've noted, there are exceptional cases that we must accommodate.)

In whatever work women do, they should receive pay equal to male peers. This is more than a matter of equity—it is a financial necessity for women who don't share a husband's paycheck, particularly if they are raising children. Women should also be trained and equipped on an equal basis with men.

In summary, I believe that the Adventist Church desperately needs women both as volunteer local elders and as salaried pastoral ministers, along with their more traditional service in health care and education. Their role would usually be nurturing and supportive rather than executive, but to fill a leadership vacuum, they are sometimes needed in senior roles. When we understand the Bible in the context of its culture, I see no reason to withhold ordination from women. I believe the church should recognize their calling from God and ordain them, not just commission them, to perform whatever pastoral function they are assigned.

This subject, while vitally important, is not necessarily a matter of eternal salvation. If you don't agree with my understanding of what the Bible says about women, that's all right. You are certainly entitled to your own convictions.

A letter from Lisa

If you are a woman and believe that God has called you to ministry, take comfort in the fact that no man can ultimately thwart heaven's purpose for your life.

Just this week I got a letter from Lisa. About six years ago my wife and I met Lisa and her husband shortly before they graduated from an Adventist college, both with theology degrees. We were impressed with this bright, talented, dedicated couple and took an interest in their future. Their dream was to work together in team pastoral ministry. But nothing opened up. Lisa began working in private-duty nursing, and her husband found a well-paying job in the business community.

As year after year went by, their dream began to fade. Somehow it didn't die. I tried to encourage them and also made some contacts on their behalf. Still nothing. Sometimes Lisa and her husband were tempted to become bitter at the system that seemed to be denying them their dream, but they managed to keep their faith in God and in this church.

Finally their prayers and patience were rewarded. Just a few days ago Lisa informed me that she's been hired as an associate pastor at one of our college churches. I wish you could see her happy letter of thanks for my recommendation, which apparently helped pave the way for her interview. Her husband's employer agreed to transfer him to a branch office in the new area, so off they go. I wish them well, and I hope that in time, the North American Division will be able to ordain Lisa for the supportive pastoral ministry to which God has called her.

I also bid success to all women, including my daughter, who dedicate their talents to the glory of God. Whether Christi ultimately chooses a career as a salaried professional or as a homemaker, I hope society will not stand in her way. I also hope that, regarding whatever plans the Lord has for her in service to Him, the Adventist Church will be waiting with open arms.

That's my prayer.

1. *The Adventist Home*, 231.
2. Ibid., 215.
3. Lisa Schwarzbaum, "Katie Did It," *Entertainment*, 31 July 1992, 30.
4. Arlene Taylor, "The Power of Words," *Adventist Review*, 2 April 1992, 24.
5. Ibid.

Chapter 8

Addicted to Affirmation

(Addiction, codependency, and self-esteem)

An unusual man he was. They called him K.B. He was a professional chameleon, an undercover policeman whose exploits in drug interdiction were so dramatic they were featured in a leading national magazine.

Time and again K.B. infiltrated underworld drug rings. He would venture boldly into the dark corners of restaurants where the bosses held court, stroll over to their table, and brazenly sit beside them. He would regale them with fabricated stories, win their confidence, and work his way into their rackets. Then, at the strategic moment, he would have them all arrested.

Needless to say, the mob didn't appreciate K.B.'s interference with their business. One night four men grabbed him and drove him at gunpoint to a Los Angeles park, where they planned to kill him. K.B. slowly slid his hand into his waistband and pulled out a small gun he kept hidden there. In several fiery seconds he shot all four of his captors and escaped once again.

K.B. could beat any odds and overcome any foe. Anyone, that is, except himself. He was hopelessly addicted to alcohol. It made him a terror around the house. Nine times he broke his wife's nose. His daughter committed suicide. His son ran away to Hollywood and drowned himself in pleasures and sorrows.

In God's providence, I met K.B.'s son and found that the Holy Spirit had prepared his heart for the gospel. It was my joy to help him find faith in Christ, explore with him the teachings of the Bible, and finally baptize him. Then one afternoon I met K.B. himself. He had come to Los Angeles to sign a movie contract about his life story. The Lord opened an opportunity for me to confront him with the gospel. Surprisingly, after initially scorning my presence, he humbled himself before God, fell to his knees in sobs, and accepted Christ. I enrolled him in a Christian detox center, where he spent most of the next month. He hoped upon release to go on the high-school circuit, telling his testimony and warning young people about the evils of addiction.

I wish K.B.'s story had a happy ending. After months of professional counseling bolstered by prayer, encouragement, and Christian fellowship, he slid back into the dark pit of addiction from which God had wonderfully saved him. Then he disappeared, and nobody could find him.

I learned a lot about addiction from working with K.B. and a number of other addicted people. They've cried and lied (often at the same time), cheated me, and threatened me. Now and then a few have triumphed in Christ. I've seen what treatment centers can do and their limitations, noticing that some addicted people seem to be helped while others aren't. The finest treatment programs in the world are no substitute for repentance and earnest cooperation by the one addicted to alcohol or drugs.

Just a disease?

There are numerous addictions to which one can get hooked. Recovery groups are sprouting everywhere for gamblers, spenders, child abusers, "workaholics," shoplifters, overeaters, and the oversexed. There's even a group called "Messies Anonymous" for people who have trouble cleaning up the kitchen! To service this massive market of escaping addicts, Hallmark has come out with a "recovery" line of fifty-one cards.

Most of us, it seems, suffer a compulsive craving for some harmful habit that at least has the potential of developing into a life-controlling addiction. Many times that addiction is to another person, often another addict. We can become so emotionally dependent upon a troubled loved one that we become "codependents" or "enablers," assisting him or her in maintaining the deceptive veneer of normalcy, that leaky umbrella under which addiction flourishes. Enablers provide the smoke screen behind which addicts mask their habits; they will lie to cover up for the addict and even bankroll the habit.

No doubt about it, there are a lot of hurting people around, suffering from one addiction or another, sometimes multiple addictions. Is their problem only a disease, or is it also a sin? The answer is important. You see, some suggest that addiction is a predetermined fate, something programmed from birth in one's genes. If that's true, how can you blame the addict simply for fulfilling his fate? But on the other hand, if addiction is behavior that can be avoided, a sin to be spurned, there is no excuse for maintaining a connection to cocaine, tobacco, alcohol, or whatever.

Picture the awful scene when my drunken friend K.B. terrorized his family, shot his gun around the house, and broke his family's bones and hearts. Was he innocent of sin in getting drunk again and again, because his addiction was supposed to be a disease? Or did he exercise his freedom of moral choice by refusing his wife's pleas to get help for himself? If he could have accepted help and didn't, how could one say he had no responsibility for his actions?

Whether recovery writers acknowledge it or not, calling a behavioral problem a "disease" can lessen one's sense of personal responsibility for engaging in that behavior. Our local newspaper yesterday reported the arrest of a paramedic for raping two women. "I'm not to blame!" he protested. "I'm sick! I wanted counseling for my sexual cravings, but my employer said funds weren't available. If I could have gotten the help I needed, I wouldn't have attacked those women."

How about that! Not guilty by reason of no counseling.

Personal responsibility

Stanton Peele in *Diseasing of America: Addiction Treatment Out of Control* observed: "Disease definitions undermine the individual's obligation to control behavior and to answer for misconduct. . . . They legitimatize, reinforce, and excuse the behaviors in question—convincing people, contrary to all evidence, that their behavior is not their own."[1]

Several years ago the U.S. Veterans Administration stirred up a hornet's nest by challenging the notion that alcoholism is a disease. Actually, it was only several decades ago that this disease concept became popular. Many Christian counselors have simply accepted the theories of secular researchers. Increasingly, however, experts are concluding that alcoholism is a problem of behavior and not merely one of disease.

Herbert Fingarette is a consultant on addiction to the World Health Organization and a researcher at the Stanford Center for Advanced Studies and Behavioral Sciences. He recently wrote the book *Heavy Drinking: The Myth of Alcoholism as a Disease.* In it he declared that regarding addiction as a disease ignores human responsibility and denies the spiritual dimension of alcohol dependency.

Fingarette observed that no scientific evidence would indicate that alcoholics can't do something about their habit. The drinker's attitude determines alcohol consumption. He asserts that no leading authorities accept the classic disease concept for alcoholism.

But don't some people have a genetic weakness for alcoholism? Very likely so. But don't all of us suffer from compulsions and predispositions to sin of one kind or another? And whenever we pander to these weaknesses, there are consequences. Addicts of any kind must accept responsibility for their behavior. There may be reasons for their addictions, but they are not helpless victims in the same way the loved ones they hurt are victimized.

One proof that addicts aren't mere victims is their typical dishonesty. Denial and manipulation lie at the heart of their problem. Ann Landers published a letter from a Florida prisoner who complained that he had been trying without success for fifteen years to get help for his addiction. How sad, many people imagined—until the prison warden wrote and set the story straight: "Mr. _____ has been incarcerated four times by the department. He was offered an opportunity to participate in a drug program while assigned to a community center but chose to escape before he was able to participate. In August 1990, he was returned to the department with a new sentence and enrolled in the auto mechanics course and the GED program. He dropped out of both programs within two weeks."

Twelve steps to responsibility

So much for that addict whom nobody wanted to help. Another letter writer wrote: "When I read that letter from the prisoner in Florida, I was irritated. His attitude is typical of addicted people. These whiners have a common failing—unwillingness to assume responsibility for their lives. Blaming someone else (in this case, the Florida prison system) will never get that guy sober.... I was in four treatment centers before I ended up doing time [in jail]. Nothing worked for me until I got with the twelve-step program of A.A. It works because it puts the responsibility where it belongs—on the user."

The famous and successful "Twelve Steps" of Alcoholics Anonymous make no mention of the word *sin*, as such, but do emphasize responsibility and moral accountability.

1. We admitted we were powerless . . . unmanageable. 2. Came to believe that a Power greater than ourselves could restore us to sanity. 3. Made a decision to turn our will and our lives over to the care of God as we understood Him. 4. Made a searching and fearless moral inventory of ourselves. 5. Admitted to God, to ourselves, and to another human being the exact moral nature of our wrongs. 6. Were entirely ready to have God remove all these defects of character. 7. Humbly asked Him to remove our shortcomings. 8. Made a list of all persons we had harmed, and . . . made direct amends to such people wherever possible.

The Twelve Steps also require the recovering addict to go to God, or whomever they believe the higher power to be, and pray for knowledge of His will and His power. The Twelve Steps make no attempt to escape blame.

It might seem compassionate to tell addicted loved ones that their problem is not their fault and encourage them to view themselves as helpless victims. But think it through. What they are really hearing us say is that they are hopeless. That's not good news at all, and it's also untrue. Addicts *can* choose to get help. And unless they do take responsibility for their addictions, they can never act responsibly.

Our original dysfunctional parents

It's about time to ask the question: Is there any word from the Lord about addiction? The Bible does not flatter human nature; it's quite blunt about the sin problem all of us suffer. "The heart is deceitful above all things, and desperately wicked" (Jeremiah 17:9). This sin problem is a type of sickness, because "the whole head is sick, and the whole heart faints" (Isaiah 1:5). So addiction can be considered a disease in the sense that all sin is a disease. Ellen White concurs:

> Among the victims of intemperance are men of all classes and all professions. . . . Unless a helping hand is held out to them, they will sink lower and lower. With these self-indulgence is not only a moral sin, but a physical disease.[2]

So addiction is *both* a physical disease and a moral sin. Sinfulness is congenital, something we received at birth. In fact, it goes back farther than the womb. Psychologists point to our parents as the source of many problems—the "dysfunctional family" is a current term. But the cause of our problems really goes back to something dysfunctional that happened in the Garden of Eden. The Bible says, "Therefore, just as through one man sin entered the world, and death through sin, and thus death spread to all men, because all sinned" (Romans 5:12). So we all sinned with Adam back there in the Garden of Eden. And because of it, we all met our death back then.

Perhaps you've noticed from your own cravings that we really aren't sinners by our own choice. In the same way that a rattlesnake strikes not by choice but by nature, so we also strike out and sin by nature. We are born sinners through Adam's sin.

"That's not fair," you may protest. "Why should God let us suffer for something we never did?" Well, God wouldn't be fair if He left us to cope with Adam's fall all by ourselves. He sent Jesus to reconcile this world, replacing condemnation with justification, that is, forgiveness: "So then as through one transgression there resulted condemnation to all men; even so through one act of righteousness there resulted justification of life to all men" (Romans 5:18, NASB).

What happened to us at Calvary counteracts what happened to us in Eden. We were "in Adam" when he sinned and brought condemnation upon the entire human family. But, thank God, we also were "in Christ" when He brought salvation to "all men."

This leaves us with an important question: If these events happened to us independently of our choice, outside our own control, what about our personal freedom of choice? Where does our decision come in? The gospel restores personal liberty. We have our choice of parents—Adam or Christ, along with our choice of history—Adam's sin or Christ's salvation. We can even choose our verdict in the judgment—Adam's condemnation or Christ's justification. When we choose Christ over Adam, we also receive the power of His victory to overcome Adam's failure.

So what happened to us at Calvary more than atoned for what happened to us in Eden. Justification of life came upon "all men"—yet not everyone will be saved and empowered. Only those who "*receive* abundance of grace and of the gift of righteousness" (Romans 5:17, emphasis supplied).

Do you see it? We had no choice about becoming sinners; we were born that way from Adam. But thank God for His solution in Christ. It's a solution to our guilt as well as a solution to our weakness.

Why addiction is condemned

God doesn't blame us for being sinners; we can be lost only if we refuse to confess and forsake our sins in exchange for God's gift of Jesus Christ. The thing that stops most addicts from getting help from God is the fundamental dishonesty bred in hopelessness that discourages them from confronting their addiction. Since deception is involved in addiction—both self-deception and deceiving others—we would expect the Bible to have some earnest warnings about such destructive behavior. And it does. In the New Testament the apostle Paul lists a number of sins, and notice what he includes along with such things as adultery and hatred: "Envy, murders, drunkenness, revelries, and the like; of which I tell you beforehand, just as I also told you in time past, that those who practice such things will not inherit the kingdom of God" (Galatians 5:21).

That's a powerful warning from the Word of God. Drunkenness is listed alongside a number of sinful practices that will disqualify us from heaven. Remember that the Lord doesn't count us guilty when we have repented of our sins and honestly come to Him for help, even when we struggle and fail. What robs us of eternal life is a stubborn refusal to confront our sins and exchange them for what Jesus offers us.

The prodigal

You know the story Christ told about the prodigal who left his father and home for a faraway land, where he wasted his life with carousing and drunkenness. At last, the Bible says, he "came to himself." That means he confronted his behavior and made his decision: "I will arise and go to my father, and will say to him, 'Father, I have sinned against heaven and before you' " (Luke 15:18).

No more self-deception and escapism! The young man assumed total responsibility for his irresponsible behavior, declaring it a sin. "I have sinned," he confessed. Then he took action by going home. His loving father ran to welcome his long-lost son, showering mercy and forgiveness upon him. He announced: "This my son was dead and is alive again; he was lost and is found" (Luke 15:24).

Did you notice? The Bible says that the son had been lost, spiritually dead. Not just diseased, but dead lost. Remember that the fundamental sin of alcoholics is not their craving to drink; that, they cannot help. Sinful desires came to us through Adam, but a solution is available in Christ. Jesus said, "If anyone thirsts, let him come to Me and drink" (John 7:37). Alcoholics will be lost only if they continue seeking refuge in the bottle instead of in Christ's living water. And drug addicts aren't lost because of their cravings, but only if they continue surrendering themselves to counterfeit fulfillment rather than to what Jesus offers them.

Self-esteem the solution?

As we might expect, secular psychologists vigorously deny that the diseased behavior of addicts has its roots in a sinful nature and the fall of humanity in Eden. They point to low self-esteem as the basic cause of addiction. If addicted persons could only enjoy a healthy self-image and learn to love themselves, the experts suggest, they would be "empowered" to overcome their addiction.

No doubt a low sense of self-worth contributes to sinful behavior. Having suffered many years of low self-esteem myself, I can testify to that. However, popular psychology through its denial of God offers the wrong approach in solving a damaged self-image.

First, let's examine the type of thinking that destroys self-esteem. Then, after examining the world's presumed remedy, we'll notice God's solution.

People feel inferior because they compare themselves with others who seem better than they are. Students in law school judge themselves inferior to a graduate who has just passed the bar exam. But this new lawyer envies an already prosperous attorney—who, in turn, feels less valuable than the mayor of the city. Of course, the mayor considers himself or herself unimportant compared with the governor. And the governor keeps hoping to be president of the United States!

The nation's leader enthroned in the White House is immune to inferiority, we might imagine. Not really! In comparing himself with great leaders of the past, such as Lincoln and Washington, even the chief executive may suffer from pangs of low self-esteem. This business of self-worth seems to be a no-win situation. There's always someone around, or in memory, more successful, more intelligent, more popular, or better looking.

This world bases self-worth on interpersonal comparisons. And we hate it. Even so, we find it hard to stop measuring each other and ourselves by the possession of these so-called qualities: "He's worth ten million." "Isn't she a doll?" "Another promotion!"

It's cruel. And it gets worse, because whatever limited success we do achieve, once earned, may not last. Today's hero can be tomorrow's castaway. The ballplayer who delights the cheering crowd with a game-winning home run can instantly forfeit his popularity with a game-losing error. There's no security in this world's value system of wealth, power, good looks, and success.

Counterfeit affirmation

In an attempt to break the cycle of negative comparisons that fosters a low self-image, it's popular now to avoid any reminder of one's deficiencies. Critical self-examination is out. Affirmation is in.

Newsweek ran an article covering the new thinking entitled: "Hey, I'm Terrific!" It told of schools with self-esteem corners and banners of self-congratulation: "We applaud ourselves." The San Diego school system even tried to abolish failing grades as a threat to self-esteem! Other schools have erupted in awards, gold stars, and happy-face stickers for completing even the most pedestrian tasks. "Celebrate Yourself" is the current mantra.

There have been measurable results; self-esteem has risen. "Psychologist Harold Stevenson of the University of Michigan found that American schoolchildren rank far ahead of students in Japan, Taiwan, and China in self-confidence about their abilities in math. Unfortunately, this achievement was marred by the fact that Americans were far behind in *actual performance* in math."[3]

Cheap affirmation has replaced wholesome self-evaluation. One publication, "101 Ways to Make Your Child Feel Special," recommends that you "tell your child how nice he or she looks . . . even if plaid pants are being worn with a striped shirt!" Have we forgotten the pursuit of excellence in this mad rush to dispense with all negative thoughts? Empty slogans have simply made a lot of arrogant nonperformers think they are great. And such a program requires little effort from teachers or parents: "Who wants to be bothered waiting for a child to do something right, when it's so much simpler just to praise him all the time?"[4]

Not only are such methods dishonest and lazy, they also don't work. The acquisitions editor for a small company that specializes in self-help affirmation books says, "You might expect that people who work for such a company would in general be terribly well-adjusted folks. . . . Think again. . . . Two in-house authors of a volume on stress are on the verge of suing each other. Our best-selling book on phobias is lacking an author cover photo because—you guessed it—the author has a phobia about having his picture taken. . . . I'm looking for a self-help book for editors of self-help books."[5]

No, self-esteem in itself is not the answer. Regardless of how much self-esteem they have, people will continue to behave poorly and suffer the consequences because they have a nature that is bent toward evil. Feeling good about themselves will not alter this depravity. Thus it is unwise to seek the solution to inappropriate behavior in self-esteem itself.

Some have suggested that a better self-image would solve the problem of teenage pregnancies. Most studies are inconclusive. One actually showed the opposite: some teens felt so good about themselves that they gained the confidence to become openly promiscuous. Evidently mere positive thinking and cheap affirmation is not the solution to our personal struggles.

God's solution to low self-esteem

We've discussed how popular psychology tends to minimize standards and just affirm everyone in whatever they happen to be doing. The Bible takes a dramatically different approach. Instead of dispensing with standards, the Bible establishes an entirely different set of values based upon the gospel. Here we find the key to genuine self-esteem. Knowing what we're worth—and why—provides a rejuvenated outlook on life.

The first thing the Bible does in restoring our sense of self-worth is to strip away the delusion that we just happened to evolve from animals. If we evolved from a puddle of chemicals that eventually developed into snails and finally into humans, no wonder secular psychologists and educators need to deceive themselves to establish self-esteem. If our ancestors crawled around in the mud without much of a brain, what does that do for us?

The Bible tells us we are created in the image of God. In fact, He created us to satisfy an emotional hunger in His own heart. Up in heaven God was surrounded by millions of angels and celestial beings, but He missed having His own children. That's why He made us, so we could be His family, bearing His unique likeness. "God created man in His own image; . . . male and female He created them" (Genesis 1:27).

Some people, even Christians, imagine that God can get along quite well all alone. After all, the Almighty should be able to take care of Himself. Actually, the glorious reality behind our creation is the fact that we exist as human beings because of the need God feels in His heart for us! This shouldn't be hard for us to understand. Husbands and wives enjoy each other and their many friends, yet still they feel a loneliness for children. So they forfeit peace and prosperity for the privilege of taking care of a screaming little red-faced dynamo—diapers and all! It's that human hunger to be parents, to have and to hold someone formed after our likeness, the craving to care for and laugh with one of our own.

Our precious children need the hugs and kisses we bestow upon them. But we need their little hugs and kisses just as much, don't you think? How would you feel if your little ones didn't hug you? We really need our children! Now think about it—what does this tell us about God and His craving for our affection?

Rather than focusing on "loving ourselves," a better idea would be to plunge ourselves into the love of God, bathing our minds in the knowledge of His affection for us. Yes, God created us for fellowship with Him. More dearly than we yearn for human love, He craves our affection, our trust, our loyalty. What a boost to our sense of self-worth.

Worth revealed at Calvary

"Wait a moment," some protest. "Agreed that God endowed us with wonderful worth at creation, making us in His image as His precious children. But then we lost our innocence, and with that we lost our worth. Didn't we?"

Not at all. Ponder this. I wear contact lenses. The other night when I turned off my computer, it was late. I was tired. When I took the contact lenses from my eyes, one of them popped away and bounced somewhere into the cat litter box. What a way to end the day!

The lens was lost. It was filthy. But it still had lost none of its

value. It was just as precious as the other lens that was "saved."
That's why I searched for it until I found it and saved it.

Likewise, when the human race plunged into the litter box of
sin, we lost none of our value. Lost, yes. Dirty, yes. But just as
precious as ever. Proof of this is the ultimate price God paid for
us at Calvary: "God so loved the world that he gave his one and
only Son, that whoever believes in him shall not perish but have
eternal life" (John 3:16, NIV).

Do you see it? God exchanged the life of His Son to ransom a
lost world. In fact, Jesus would have died just for you or for me.
The apostle Paul said, "I live by faith in the Son of God, who
loved *me* and gave Himself for *me*" (Galatians 2:20, emphasis
supplied). You know, it's one thing to believe Jesus died for the
whole world, but it's especially wonderful to realize He died for
me personally—and for you. That's how precious you are in the
sight of God.

Christ's life exchanged for yours! So your heavenly Father
considers you equal in value to His Son Jesus. That seems impossible, but Christ Himself recognized this fact when He prayed
for His disciples, "You . . . have loved them even as [as much as]
You have loved Me" (John 17:23).

When I first learned this, I couldn't believe it. How could God
consider me so valuable, sinful as I am? Then it dawned on me
that my importance to God is not based upon my spiritual con-
dition or my accomplishments. If that were true, the Lord could
have no relationship with any of us, for "all have sinned and fall
short of the glory of God" (Romans 3:23).

Think about it. When a car gets wrecked, wrapped around a
tree, it loses its value. Not so with human beings. When the
human race wrecked at the tree in the Garden of Eden and
became defiled by sin, we remained every bit as valuable to God
as before. Doomed to certain death, but precious just the same.

Incredible but true, God loves us as much as He loves Jesus!
As long as we keep this in mind, is it possible to feel inferior at
all to anyone, anywhere?

No, the Lord doesn't find it necessary to flatter us in restoring
our self-esteem. The Bible offers no affirmation whatsoever of
our sinful characters. On the contrary, the Bible plainly declares

us to be lost sinners without hope in ourselves. The measure of our worth is the person of Jesus Christ.

I wish more Christian treatment programs for addicts would emphasize this gospel truth. Many detox centers, determined to treat alcoholism as a disease instead of a sin, have become so sophisticated in the wisdom of this world that they fail to offer salvation in Christ. I'm not suggesting that they impose the gospel on anybody, but at least they could make Jesus available. Without Him, our quest for self-esteem becomes an exercise in self-deception. It's the loving grace of God that gives us courage to honestly confess our sins and confront them.

There remains, of course, a lifelong struggle to maintain our faith relationship with Christ rather than reverting to our cravings. That's the bad news. The good news is that one happy day Jesus will return from heaven to rescue us from this troubled planet and transform our corrupt natures into incorruption while He exchanges our mortality for immortality (see 1 Corinthians 15:51-55).

Adopted by Abba

Noted secular psychiatrist Stanley Greenspan observed that a wholesome self-image is based upon (1) a need for a constant and loving caregiver and (2) a fundamental sense of security and safety.[6] Is it any surprise that this is exactly what our loving heavenly Father offers us? Through His gift of Jesus Christ, we find acceptance and adoption. "You did not receive a spirit that makes you a slave again to fear, but you received the Spirit of sonship. And by him [Jesus] we cry, 'Abba, Father' " (Romans 8:15, NIV).

That word *Abba* is interesting. Some would translate it "father," but Paul could have chosen a more formal word if that's what he wanted to say. *Abba* actually signifies the affectionate, familiar name for father—"Daddy!" At first we might shrink from such familiarity with Almighty God. It seems somehow irreverent. Then it dawns on us that this word *Abba* precisely describes the close paternal relationship we may have been missing all our lives. And remember, the affectionate faith relationship we have with our "Abba" in heaven does more than merely meet our own needs—it's for God's sake too. It's reassuring to know that He needs our love as well.

In this wonderful relationship with Him we receive all the power we need to bid farewell both to addictive behavior and to low self-esteem.

---

1. Quoted by Ron Rhodes, "Recovering From the Recovery Movement," *Christian Research Journal*, Summer 1992, 10.

2. *Ministry of Healing*, 172.

3. "Hey, I'm Terrific," *Newsweek*, 17 February 1992, 48.

4. Ibid., 49.

5. Barbara Quick, "Tales From the Self-Help Mill," *Newsweek*, 31 August 1992, 14.

6. *Newsweek*, 17 February 1992, 48.

Chapter 9

Homelessness and Heartlessness

(Poverty and wealth)

A rusty, old lowrider chugged up our church driveway in Anaheim, California. Its cargo of homeless refugees stumbled into my office. Obviously, they hadn't bathed in many days. Forty-five minutes after they left, my secretary was still running around, spraying air deodorizer. Soon they would be back, begging for more help.

What should we do about the homeless? We can't just ignore them and hope they will go away. They need an apartment and employment. But suppose they can't hold a job or just won't work? Should Christians support them in wasting away their lives?

Two thousand years ago Jesus predicted, "You have the poor with you always" (Mark 14:7). That's true now more than ever. Each year seventy million of our brothers and sisters die of starvation. Every night one billion of them go to bed hungry. Actually, they don't even have beds; they just roll out their grass mats and curl up with their hunger pangs. Even the United States, land of plenty, has an estimated thirty-five million poor people, at least half a million of whom are homeless.

An unfair situation

One fact should be obvious right from the start. In this suffering world, selfishness and greed amount to obscenity. In many nations the wealthy prey upon the poor. Even in the United

States, "if one counts a broad range of federal spending and tax programs, an average upper-income person will get more [government benefits] than a typical poor person."[1] Consider housing. "Counting the mortgage interest and other homeownership tax breaks, the government spends more than four times as much on middle- and upper-income families as it does to house the poor."[2] Add to that subsidized health care, since the government doesn't tax health-care benefits that employers pay workers. "While the government certainly spent a lot last year [1991] on health care for the poor (roughly $50 billion), it 'spent' even more—$65 billion—on this tax subsidy."[3]

All things considered, "the average person with an income over $100,000 receives cash benefits (like social security) of $5,688, slightly greater than those of someone with less than $10,000 in income, according to a study by the conservative National Taxpayers Union Foundation, which used unpublished data from the Congressional Budget Office [CBO]."[4] "Another unpublished CBO analysis obtained by *Newsweek* revealed that in 1989 at least $11 billion was spent on people with incomes above $100,000."[5]

In agriculture, wealthy farmers receive crop and dairy subsidies that can add up to more than $100,000 a year. Others receive subsidized water benefits worth a staggering amount. In one recent year, just one grower, Panoche Farms in California, received water subsidies that cost taxpayers more than $550,000. What's more, much of that water went to grow cotton, a subsidized crop.

Consider the elderly. Although many suffer poverty, on average they are the wealthiest group of all Americans. Yet the government spends four times as much on senior citizens as on children, who have the greatest needs. "In 1989 the government spent more for the medical care of well-off seniors than it did on Head Start, job training, and WIC [women, infants, and children nutrition subsidies] *combined*."[6]

Do you see what's happening? The wealthy hire lobbyists and throw their money behind candidates who will reward them with tax breaks and gold-plated benefits.

How does God feel about the situation? No need to guess.

Warning to the greedy

The Bible proclaims a stern warning to wealthy people who have no heart for the poor: "Come now, you rich, weep and howl for your miseries that are coming upon you! . . . Your gold and silver are corroded, and their corrosion will be a witness against you and will eat your flesh like fire. You have heaped up treasure in the last days. . . . You have lived on the earth in pleasure and luxury; you have fattened your hearts as in a day of slaughter" (James 5:1-5).

Greed is one of the greatest sins of our age, and it even flourishes among religious people. You may recall Christ's story about the wealthy man who had stockpiled for his own selfish pleasure while ignoring the suffering of poverty around him. There's nothing in Christ's story to indicate this man was dishonest or dishonorable. No doubt he was admired and respected in the community. He worked hard for his money, and he imagined he could do with it anything he pleased. "But God said to him, 'You fool! This night your soul will be required of you; then whose will those things be which you have provided?' So is he who lays up treasure for himself, and is not rich toward God" (Luke 12:20, 21).

This poor rich man hoarded his surplus, and his greed cost him his life. He refused to acknowledge the purpose for which God had so abundantly blessed his labors. Not so that he might stash wealth away for himself, but rather so he could share.

Politically correct greed has even infected the Adventist Church. Wealthy members imagine that if they faithfully return tithes and offerings, the remainder is theirs to spend as they please. They flatter themselves that they are quite generous, forgetting the lesson of the widow's mites: the Lord judges our stewardship not by how much we give but by how much we keep back for ourselves.

Often wealthy members demand power in the church in exchange for their tax-deductible gifts. They seek to rule the body of Christ with a golden fist. Pastors and conference presidents are often afraid of them. I remember one wealthy physician whose friend, an immoral teacher, was corrupting the spiritual atmosphere of an academy. When I stood up to him on behalf of concerned parents, he became furious. I think he wanted to send me to Antarctica to evangelize the penguins!

I know of members wearing Rolex watches who will condemn a pregnant woman for quietly wearing a wedding ring to show that she is married. They accuse her of sinful adornment! Is there no such thing as adorning one's bank account? Or adorning one's home? Or adornment on wheels?

I'm just asking questions. Let's not presume to judge wealthy families. Maybe they are far more generous than we know, and the Lord keeps them wealthy so they can keep giving. I know some extremely wealthy people who give huge gifts to the Lord's work, only to have the Lord give it right back. Evidently He intends to make them a continuing resource for His church, and they are good and faithful servants.

Only God is worthy to judge anyone's faithfulness. And all of us are going to give account to Him for our own stewardship. Indeed we will. According to Jesus, some of us will wake up a thousand years too late and hear the awful condemnation, "Depart from Me, you cursed, into the everlasting fire prepared for the devil and his angels: for I was hungry and you gave Me no food. . . . Assuredly, I say to you, inasmuch as you did not do it to one of the least of these, you did not do it to Me" (Matthew 25:41-45).

A powerful warning, and Christ meant every word of it. The way we treat the poor is an important barometer of our spirituality and a test of our faithfulness. How can we know if we are guilty of greed? I suggest you pray about it and counsel with your pastor.

Poverty doesn't mean piety

Let's not become needlessly anxious on this matter of stewardship. The Lord recognizes any sincere commitment to be faithful, and He is reasonable. While we must not put our trust in wealth, the Bible also says that God "gives us richly all things to enjoy" (1 Timothy 6:17). So there is nothing wrong with enjoying the basic comforts of life.

Some social liberals seem determined to heap guilt upon all who live in comfortable homes, making heroes out of people just because they are poor. But poverty is not necessarily connected to piety. There aren't too many Mother Teresas around. Some of the most greedy people you meet are poor. They don't want less than the rich want; it's just that some of them are too lazy to discipline themselves to earn a living. They prefer to take their welfare scraps and flush them away in the lottery, indulging vain fantasies of wealth.

Notice what the Bible says in this sampling from the Proverbs:

He who tills his land will have plenty of bread, but he who follows frivolity will have poverty enough! (28:19).

Do not love sleep, lest you come to poverty; open your eyes, and you will be satisfied with bread (20:13).

The drunkard and the glutton will come to poverty, and drowsiness will clothe a man with rags (23:21; see also 6:10, 11 and 18:9).

Of course, these proverbs are general principles, not ironclad guarantees. I know some decent, industrious people who have found themselves homeless through such adverse circumstances as illness, a death in the family, or a job layoff. Such unfortunate victims deserve our helping hand.

Some homeless people, however, actually seem to prefer life on the streets. Conditions may be harsh there, but there are also pleasant trade-offs: no rent to pay, no responsibilities, and no accountability to anyone. Many of the homeless diligently seek work, but others would rather beg and scavenge the dumpsters.

Some guilt-ridden Christians feel compelled to dispense indiscriminate aid to everyone who requests it because they misinterpret something Jesus said: "Give to him who asks you, and from him who wants to borrow from you do not turn away" (Matthew 5:42). Did the Lord intend these words to mean that we must subsidize laziness with blind generosity? Not on the basis of everything else we read in the Bible. Here's how the inspired apostle Paul addressed the lazy poor in his day: "When we were with you, we commanded you this: If anyone will not work, neither shall he eat" (2 Thessalonians 3:10).

Does this sound cruel? It's not cruel; it's tough love. Pandering to panhandlers may seem compassionate, but it's actually demeaning and immoral. The Lord does not want us to become enablers of idleness and sloth. Emergency situations happen, and it becomes necessary to administer direct relief. In normal circumstances, however, the biblical way of helping the poor is to empower them to help themselves.

There should be no need to have beggars roaming our streets. Their harassment is annoying, frightening, and sometimes dangerous. Living on the street is also dangerous to the homeless themselves and degrading to their self-esteem. Society should offer them opportunity to provide for themselves whenever possible. In Bible times God required farmers to leave behind the gleanings of their fields so the poor could come and sustain themselves (see Leviticus 19:10). How can we make similar provisions for today's poor and homeless?

The Good Samaritan solution

First, we should resist lumping the poor all into one vast group. The homeless include the mentally ill, most of whom are addicted to alcohol or drugs; single adults; runaway youth; battered wives with their children; and unemployed families.

Teenage runaways often become victims of pimps and drug dealers. We need to help them find placement in homes. If their own families are abusive, incestuous, or otherwise dysfunctional, foster families are their lifeline to the future. Many sexually abused girls know only how to relate to men in a promiscuous and seductive manner. It takes foster fathers of tremendous integrity to provide the pure paternal love they really need. Here is one area in which consecrated Christian families can do a world of good.

Countless volunteer agencies shelter battered women and their children who need a temporary refuge. Christian homes can also be a safehouse for the victims of domestic civil war, helping them recover and pull their lives back together. The Bible commands us to care for the homeless and "bring to your house the poor who are cast out" (Isaiah 58:7).

Suppose your home is too small, however. Or perhaps both spouses work during the day and having another family living in your home would be too disruptive. One solution is to help your church establish a Good Samaritan Club for housing battered women with children or other types of homeless families. Each club could be comprised of ten sponsors willing to donate seventy-five dollars a month, which pays for an apartment rented for the homeless family. Meanwhile, the church as a whole makes intensive efforts to help the parents find employment. During the first month, the club pays the total rent for the family. In the second month, the family assumes half the rent from new employment income. The third month, 75 percent. And by the fourth month the family is on its own, fully independent financially.

The Good Samaritan program solves a terrible dilemma homeless families suffer. Without first and last months' rent paid in advance, they can't get an apartment. But they have no money, and nobody will hire them without a permanent address. While they are trapped in this vicious cycle, job opportunities go by, because they have no residence as a base from which to work. The Good Samaritan program meets these challenges, offering homeless families a real opportunity to get back on their feet.

I think you can see the tremendous value of such a program, but you can also see the tremendous potential for abuse. Many homeless people are world-class manipulators—and are dangerous as well. My wife and I have been lied to, cheated, and robbed by people we've tried to help. How do Christians (and the church) guard against being taken advantage of?

There must be a thorough interview with a counselor or the pastor. If anything sounds suspicious, require proof to back up the story—doctor's papers, various types of identification, pay stubs from former employment, etc. If the family claims to have lost such evidence, help them call for duplicates. If they say they have been robbed, require a police report of their lost goods. Only by carefully safeguarding from abuse can the program survive and thrive.

Uncle Sam must help

The Good Samaritan plan, wonderful as it is, has limitations.

The needs of many homeless people require government intervention. About 40 percent of homeless people are either mentally ill or addicts who need specialized help. The mentally ill who are unable to function and support themselves require institutional care. Authorities should gently take them off the streets and place them under restrictive but compassionate care in a state hospital—no matter how loudly and vigorously they protest.

Addicts are usually masters of manipulation, often with criminal tendencies. In my opinion, private families should not attempt to shelter them, nor should society feel obligated to provide fancy treatment centers costing a thousand dollars a day. It isn't wise, either, to build community shelters where residents can come and go and do as they please as if they were tourists staying in a hotel. Homeless addicts need medical care combined with tough-love counseling that teaches them discipline and responsibility.

Where could these services be efficiently and effectively provided? Think of all the army bases closing down because of military cutbacks. Why not fix them up to house the homeless? Provide life's basic necessities: a warm and dry shelter, a bed with a privacy curtain, nutritious food, counseling, and quality job training. While they learn a marketable trade, pay them for part-time work around the base so they can save up for an apartment of their own.

Whether they are addicts or not, single homeless people can rebuild their lives on these renovated army bases. So can families not covered by some type of private Good Samaritan program. Build private rooms for families on former army bases. Nothing fancy, but at least something that can serve as temporary living places until they become equipped to move back into the community.

Learning life's ABCs

I believe that homeless people in recovery, whether on army bases or in Good Samaritan apartments, should be required to attend a seminar on the ABCs of managing personal finances:

A. Absolutely essential expenditures for immediate needs including food, housing, medical care, transportation to work, bills due, and taxes. These are basic nonnegotiables without which we would suffer or be sued.

B. Beneficial expenditures that make life more comfortable or provide for the family's long-term needs: savings, liquidating debt not immediately due, clothing, vacations, and basic furnishings. Category B would include reasonable supplements to the bare necessities allowed in category A—things such as butter on the bread (better make that light margarine), buying a house rather than renting, a more reliable car, or a night out with the spouse and/or kids.

C. Cravings that aren't sinful extravagance. Such a legitimate wish list might include a new car, replacements for the cat-scratched furniture, or a larger house with an extra bedroom. Maybe even a family trip to the Holy Land someday. But first things first. Not a dime should be spent on a B category item until everything in A is paid for.

Churches could hold seminars in financial management—there's a lot of good religion in managing the resources God entrusts to us. Methodist founder John Wesley advised: *Earn* all you can, then *save* all you can, so you can *give* all you can.

Above all, we should return to God the tithe—that is Category A+—along with offerings as we are able. Progressing from financial bankruptcy to having a surplus for sharing with others does wonders for one's sense of well-being. Emotional healing is accelerated when we become helpers instead of just consumers.

The ultimate solution to low self-esteem is understanding and accepting our infinite value in the eyes of God. Total healing for the soul and spirit comes through a personal relationship with God through Christ, a friendship that leads us to trust and obey. When we thus entrust our lives to God, He has a surprise for us. He makes us "joint heirs with Christ" so that everything Jesus owns belongs to us too (Romans 8:17). As Christians we "inherit all things" for eternity (Revelation 21:7).

Global solutions

The solutions mentioned in this chapter are needed around the world. Because of civil war, corrupt politicians, religious fatalism, or basic ignorance of how to make use of what is already available, many nations are chronically poor despite an abundance of fertile soil, water, and natural resources.

Because millions are starving, immediate emergency relief is needed. The permanent solution, however, is not tossing these starving people a fish, but teaching them to fish for themselves. Here is where the Adventist Development and Relief Agency is doing a magnificent work. ADRA is one of the most efficient and effective agencies for restoring primitive prosperity to impoverished areas around the world. It is fully worthy of your sacrificial support.

Providing physical relief is just the first step; we must also share the mercy and truth of Jesus Christ, who is the bread and water of eternal life. Since charity begins at home, local church outreach and nurture programs deserve your primary attention. Then comes your conference evangelism fund, followed by the various outreach ministries of the church.

Don't believe any rumors you may hear about wasted money in any of these church evangelistic ministries. For eight years I served on various committees at the Adventist Media Center, and I can assure you that every dollar is spent carefully.

Seventh-day Adventists can be humbly proud of all our denominational ministries. I know their leaders, and I can assure you that they will use your donations wisely for the glory of God and the advancement of His kingdom.

After Jesus comes there will be no more poverty. Till then, may God help us share with others as He has shared with us.

---

1. Steven Waldman, "Benefits 'R' Us," *Newsweek*, 10 August 1992, 56.
2. Ibid.
3. Ibid., 57.
4. Ibid., 56.
5. Ibid., 57.
6. Ibid., 56.

Chapter 10

Ecology or Ecomania?

(Environmental stewardship)

I'm an animal lover—cats mostly. Our family gets enormous enjoyment from the felines that have the run of our home. Much of this book has been written with Louie curled on my lap, squeezed next to my laptop computer. And when he's not lounging around the family, he's chasing after Bambi, his fellow Siamese and favorite concubine. His main goal in life is to keep her barefoot and pregnant. She just had her third batch of kittens this year—nine of them this time; a total of twenty-two born since January. Someone suggested I set up a nationwide toll-free hotline: 1-800-BUY-CATS.

Those of you who help provide room and board to America's fifty-four million cats will be delighted to know that next year—if the world can wait—I'm coming out with a devotional book especially for cat lovers. Really. The fascinating world of cats contains many lessons that can enhance your personal relationship with Jesus.

You don't believe that reading about my cats can help you live closer to the Lord? Wait and see.

One thing about cats: They don't usually come when you call. They prefer to take a message and get back to you later. Our Louie is different. Although he often ignores the rest of the family, he runs into the room like an eager puppy whenever my son Steve calls. Louie's whole life revolves around Steve; they are the best of friends. They even have a way of talking back and forth.

The Louie we have now is our second Siamese by that name. Louie the First had similar looks and habits, and he also preferred Steve above the rest of the family. The night he died, it was almost as if we had lost a member of the family. For a week we were nearly inconsolable. Steve suffered the most.

Coyotes killed our Louie. Domestic cats are a favorite supper-time snack of these canine predators that roam the hills and invade backyards under the protection of law. Three of our beloved cats died between the jaws of coyotes. We tried to keep them safe in the house, but you know how cats like to roam outdoors. One evening my wife watched in horror as a dark gray form with pointed ears crept into our yard. She could only scream as the beast bounded off with our Fluffy.

Our neighbors lost at least fourteen cats to coyotes. Dozens of children were grieving over their precious pets, gone forever. Cats and small dogs became an endangered species on our street. Why? Because radical environmentalists insist upon protecting coyotes at any cost.

If a coyote invades your property to kill your pet and you counterattack the beast, you're in trouble with the law. I'm wondering why, in the value system of many environmentalists, family pets are not as worthy of protection as wild predators? Is it possible that their ecological fervor has itself gone wild? Ecomania, you might call it—a well-intended but irrational defense of the environment.

Please understand that I'm all for preserving nature and its varied inhabitants. Those who poison our quality of life by reckless abuse of the environment deserve prosecution and stiff fines. Pollution is a sin against society and its Creator. We Christians should be at the forefront of concern for the planet He has entrusted to our care. Remember, Adam and Eve were commissioned to tend and keep their garden home (see Genesis 2:15). If that doesn't seem important, consider what will happen at the end of the world: "The nations were angry, and Your wrath has come, and the time of the dead, that they should be judged, and that You should reward Your servants the prophets and the saints, and those who fear Your name, small and great, and should *destroy those who destroy the earth"* (Revelation 11:18, emphasis supplied).

The other extreme

So the Lord wants us to take seriously the stewardship of our planet and its resources. But let's not go to ecological extremes. Some have even gone over the brink into environmental terrorism. You've probably heard about activists who drive hidden metal spikes into trees that are to be logged. Their object is to snap the blade of the saw, even though they know this endangers the lives of loggers and lumber mill employees.

Now, most environmentalists are gentle, caring people. However, some who would never endanger someone's life by spiking a tree would rather see thousands of loggers lose their jobs and have their families displaced than to allow some owls in the forest to be displaced. What's going on there? Are animals more important than people?

Yes, says one extremist group, the Voluntary Human Extinction Movement founded by antipopulation crusader Les Knight. The *Reader's Digest* reported his suggestion that total human extinction is the only long-term answer to the planet's environmental woes. Knight wants all of us to get ourselves sterilized so the earth will eventually be left to the animals.[1]

Sorry, my friend, but the Lord gave the earth and its animals to people. He gave us dominion over the animals, not the other way around (see Genesis 1:26). (I'll have to remind our cats of that.) Let's remember, though, that we are not the lords of earth, but its managers, entrusted with the care of this planet.

New Age ecovangelism

We can be thankful that most environmental activists stop short of ecomania, although many of them flirt with the impractical and illogical. For example, one of the major ecological concerns at present is protecting dolphins from being trapped in tuna nets. I do feel bad about those poor dolphins, but what about the tunas that get caught? (Don't tell my carnivorous cats that I'm questioning the source of their preferred dietary delight.) Why don't we see activists marching along Pacific Coast Highway in Malibu shouting "Save the Tunas!"?

The reason is that many New Age environmentalists actually regard dolphins as a form of life higher even than humans. They suggest that dolphins are more sensitive than most of us, spiritually alert, and eager to communicate with humans. If you buy that, then the next time a wife thinks her husband doesn't communicate enough, she should consider going down to the city aquarium and exchanging grunts and squeals with the resident dolphins. Does that sound emotionally and spiritually inspiring?

New Age religion is the driving force behind radical environmentalism. Much of Hollywood's ecomania has its roots in a pagan spiritual agenda. Some of these ecomaniacs almost deify dolphins along with their supreme goddess, Mother Earth. Many New Age ecovangelists have adopted the nature worship of the Indians, or Native Americans, to be politically correct. (By the way, calling the original residents of our continent "Native Americans" may be in vogue now, but it doesn't avoid mislabeling them with Westernism. You see, the word *American* comes courtesy of the Italian explorer Amerigo Vespucci. So we had better come up with a different name for the people who lived on this continent before the rest of us did.)

Many New Age environmentalists despise Western culture and rarely miss an opportunity to make nonnative Americans feel ashamed of their culture and lifestyle. Stanford elitists chant, "Hey, hey, ho, ho, Western culture's got to go." We can't deny that modern society's wasteful habits are regrettable, and we'll discuss in this chapter practical ways of doing better. Meanwhile, let's not drown ourselves in self-deprecation. After all, whose conscience (and agricultural wealth) feeds much of the world? When there is a famine anywhere, who comes to the rescue with plane loads of plastic-wrapped bales of food?

Plastic! Forgive me, that's another bad word in the narrow mind-set of ecomania. It's nonbiodegradable, and it's also a petroleum product. Radical environmentalists profess eagerness to reduce the use of oil and gas, but I don't see too many of them riding around on horses for nonrecreational purposes. On the contrary.

Consider the case of Tom Cruise, actor and ecovangelist who

was recently lecturing a press conference about conserving earth's natural resources. Isn't this the same actor who starred in *Days of Thunder*, playing the part of a profligate race car driver? What could be more environmentally inefficient and reckless than roaring around in a race car?

Such inconsistency pollutes the entire ecomania agenda. A while back it was a sacred duty around Hollywood to NOT FLUSH THE TOILET OFTEN in order to save water. Many actors raised quite a stink about that, forgetting perhaps that their huge swimming pools waste far more water through spillage, evaporation, and drainage than I could ever waste flushing my humble W.C.

Speaking of sewage, the whole entertainment industry is in dire need of a thorough flushing. As badly as the air is polluted over Los Angeles, the airwaves of our nation are even worse. If Hollywood's ecovangelists would quit preaching to us and adopt the pure and wholesome standards of Christianity, America would become a cleaner place in every way.

Myths of ecomania

Many of us feel so guilty about the lectures we get from ecovangelists that we never stop to question their assumptions and assertions. For example, they denounce artificial packaging as wasteful. In reality, much packaging actually reduces or prevents certain kinds of waste. One article cited a University of Arizona study showing that in Mexico, where packaging is less prevalent than in the United States, the average household throws away three times more food debris than Americans do. How can that be? "When food is processed and packaged in the United States, by-products such as rinds and peels are often used as fuel, animal feed, or in other economically useful ways."[2] Packaging also reduces spoilage, thus averting waste.

Another myth is that nonbiodegradable products, particularly plastics, are bad. Actually, most modern landfills are capped, which limits biodegradation of anything, even paper. Plastics are lighter and thus more efficient than many other forms of packaging. A German research organization assessed the result of eliminating all plastic packaging and concluded that "energy consumption would almost double and the weight of solid wastes would increase 404 percent."[3] Plastics take the least energy to manufacture of all nonrecycled containers and contribute only 8 percent of our waste by weight. Juice boxes have been a special target of environmentalists, but actually, they can save energy because they are lighter and more compact than glass bottles, and they don't need refrigeration as do plain waxpaper cartons.

Still another questionable ecologism cited in the *Reader's Digest* article is the belief that recycling deserves much greater emphasis. I believe we should be doing more of it, but let's not get carried away. "Some recycling programs use large amounts of energy and produce high volumes of water waste." Moreover, "curbside garbage-recycling programs often require more collection trucks—which means more fuel consumption and more air pollution."[4] Let's remember that much of the recycling that makes sense has already been happening. More than fifty million tons of scrap iron and steel is recycled yearly, along with sixteen million tires and mountains of glass and plastic.

One more myth of radical ecologists is that disposable diapers are environmentally evil. Junior has become politically incorrect if he crawls around in anything but cloth. The former governor of Vermont actually proposed banning disposable diapers! Actually, it's questionable whether cloth diapers are environmentally better. They "use about three times as much energy and cause nine times as much air pollution. Also, cloth diapers have to be washed in hot water, which requires further energy and generates pollution. For families using diaper services, the delivery trucks burn fuel and create fumes."[5]

Well, that's enough about the problems and inconsistencies of mistaken environmentalism. Let's look for a real solution to pollution.

Solution to pollution

Whatever the merits of disposable diapers, we can't deny that finding landfills for them and other waste products is a serious problem. Costs have skyrocketed. Incineration is an option, but it generates air pollution and leaves up to 25 percent of its mass in toxic ash. A proven and nonpolluting alternative is offered by the Burr Corporation. This company has devised an ingenious method of converting 95 percent of household waste into safe, rich fertilizer.

Here's how the patented process works. Raw solid waste comes in by garbage trucks and is dumped in a hopper. A quick sorting process removes toxic waste such as batteries and items that can be recycled such as aluminum and steel. Toxic waste, which amounts to 5 percent of total trash, is disposed of properly. The other 95 percent of garbage is useful. Recyclables amount to 15 percent. The remaining 80 percent is crushed and shredded in a series of powerful grinders. Everything—tires, refrigerators, glass, wood, rubber, and rags—gets chewed up. Next, a bacterial inoculant is sprayed on the shredded waste to accelerate decomposition. Then it travels on a conveyor belt to a temperature-controlled "window area" where decomposition (digestion from the bacteria and its enzymes) takes place. For twelve to twenty days the pulverized waste is methodically turned and mixed. After being cured at a sterilizing temperature of 170 degrees F., the material is conveyed to another grinder. Then it goes through a shaker screening process. Oversize material is sifted out and ground up again. What's left over is a grainy, brown, soil-like substance. The Burr Corporation calls the product "Burrtilizer," which is bagged and sold as fertilizer, soil conditioner, or plant food. The stuff is incredible.

After extensive testing and commercial use, turning garbage into Burrtilizer appears to be as close to a perfect environmental solution as possible. The process is approved by the Environmental Protection Agency, and the product is approved by the U.S. Department of Agriculture. The whole production is free of smoke, odor, water or air pollution, flies, rats, or other disease enhancers. No landfill or the distant transporting of garbage is necessary. Indissoluble plastics and metals become a nontoxic filler that aerates the soil. The end result is a salable, highly useful product with numerous essential micronutrients such as magnesium, zinc, sulfur, manganese, iron, copper, and boron, all of which nurture plant growth.

If you've visited Walt Disney World lately, many of the flowers you saw were blooming in Burrtilizer. Other progressive corporations are using the product, and municipalities are signing on as well. (For more information contact the Burr Corporation, 2600 E. Commercial Boulevard, Suite 200-E, Fort Lauderdale, Florida 33308. And no—I receive no financial recompense of any kind for publicizing Burr's process or product.)

The Burr Corporation's process would be terrific if all it did was avoid the need for trucking or incinerating garbage. However, not only does it eliminate the pollution associated with disposing of garbage, but when the process is finished, there is a useful, profitable product.

You may wish to encourage your local government to contact the Burr corporation. Unfortunately, incineration is big business these days, and there are often political obstacles to even the most sensible and responsible pollution solutions. Whether or not your community does something significant about pollution, here's something you can do on a personal level.

Quit eating cows

How about becoming a vegetarian? Despite the bad example of my cats, I've been one for twenty-two years. I did it for health reasons. However in researching this article, I've come to realize that a meatless diet makes a lot of environmental sense as well.

According to John Robbins of Baskin-Robbins ice-cream fame and president of EarthSave Foundation, widespread vegetarianism could feed the hungry all around the world. Just in the United States, livestock consume enough grain and soybeans to feed more than five times our population. They eat 80 percent of the corn we grow and more than 95 percent of our oats.[6]

To understand the implications of those statistics, consider this. Sustaining a meat eater's diet for one year takes three and a quarter acres of cropland. A lacto-ovovegetarian diet (a vegetarian diet plus dairy products and eggs) requires half an acre. To sustain a pure vegetarian, you only need one sixth of an acre.[7]

Vegetarianism solves other environmental problems. Annual soil erosion causes an incredible loss of farmland, stripping away enough topsoil to more than cover the state of Connecticut. Turning garbage into Burrtilizer all over the nation is a partial solution. Even more effective would be vegetarianism, since 85 percent of topsoil loss is directly associated with livestock.

Timber is another precious natural resources. Did you know that for each acre cut down to build parking lots, roads, houses, and shopping malls, seven acres of forest are cut to support livestock?[8] The South American rain forests are being decimated largely to support raising cattle for meat, much of which is exported to the United States.

No natural resource is more important to our environment than pure water. More than half our total water consumption goes toward irrigating and growing feed for livestock.To produce a single pound of meat takes about 2,500 gallons of water—the same amount that an average family uses in a month. "It takes up to 100 times more water to produce a pound of meat as it does to produce a pound of wheat. . . . If the cost of water . . . [needed by cattle ranches] were not subsidized, the cheapest hamburger meat would cost more than \$35 a pound!"[9]

Without question, one of the best things you can do for the environment is to become a vegetarian. For more than a century, Seventh-day Adventists have had special information on this matter. Are we living up to the light as well as we could be?

Our blessed hope

The world scene is an environmental horror show. The Exxon *Valdez* disaster was bad enough, but then along came the incredible environmental terrorism of Saddam Hussein in Kuwait. Capitalism frequently bears all the blame for pollution, and certainly the United States and other Western nations have much to be ashamed about. But if you've never visited a Communist country, you're in for a shock. Eastern Germany, recovering from four decades of abuse, looks like a bleak moonscape compared with the capitalized West.

Thanks to our poor stewardship, the earth everywhere is growing old like a garment. But, thank God, this polluted old planet will soon be purified. At the second coming of Jesus:

the heavens will pass away with a great noise, and the elements will melt with fervent heat; both the earth and the works that are in it will be burned up. Therefore, since all these things will be dissolved, what manner of persons ought you to be in holy conduct and godliness, looking for and hastening the coming of the day of God, because of which the heavens will be dissolved being on fire, and the elements will melt with fervent heat? Nevertheless we, according to His promise, look for new heavens and a new earth in which righteousness dwells (2 Peter 3:10-13).

Yes, Jesus is coming. Meanwhile, as the children of God still stuck on this planet, let us live holy lives. Not just in spiritual deeds and doctrine, but also in a pure and unpolluted lifestyle.

New Agers know nothing of our blessed hope. This old world is their last hope, their only hope. How painful it must be for them to see it ruined. Let's affirm their legitimate concerns while avoiding their extremes. Let's also set a good example as stewards of our God-given planet. If we are faithful, we can lift the eyes of millions to the loving God of heaven and to personal salvation in Jesus Christ. Many will then join with us in looking forward to the Saviour's soon return.

---

1. "That's Outrageous!" *Reader's Digest*, April 1992, 147.

2. Lynn Scarlett, "Don't Buy These Environmental Myths," *Reader's Digest*, May 1992, 100.

3. Ibid., 102.

4. Ibid., 101.

5. Robert J. Samuelson, "The Great Diaper Debate," *Reader's Digest*, August 1990, 120.

6. John Robbins, "Can You Have Your Environment—and Eat It Too?" *Vibrant Life*, May/June 1992, 14.

7. Ibid.

8. Ibid.

9. Ibid.

They're Back!

More Adventist Hot Potatoes is a continuation of Martin Weber's quest to find balance in the issues that tend to make church members a little hot under the collar.

With charity and an open mind, Weber asks:

- Is Adventist education still a good investment?
- Can anything good come from independent ministries?
- Do Adventist hospitals still promote our health message?
- Did Jesus feel like sinning?

Don't skip this second helping of hot potatoes.

US$8.95/Cdn$10.75. Paper.

To order, call toll free 1-800-765-6955, or visit your local ABC.

Books You Just Can't Put Down

MORE ADVENTIST HOT POTATOES

Legalistic Education

Nature of Christ

Independent Ministries

Health System

Martin Weber

The Danger Within
by Manuel Vasquez

Don't bother locking your doors to ward off the intrusion of the New Age movement—it has already been ushered into your house as a welcomed guest. Through TV, Christian meditation, electronic games and toys, and alternative health care, the New Age movement has disguised itself to hit us where we're most vulnerable.

The Danger Within uncovers the New Age's subtle impact on our lives and homes. More than psychics and channelers, crystals and horoscopes, Vasquez's research will reveal how this movement is setting the stage for Satan's grand deception.

US$8.95/Cdn$12.10. Paper.

Available at your local ABC, or call toll free 1-800-765-6955.

Books You Just Can't Put Down
from Pacific Press

© 1993 Pacific Press Publishing Association 490/9832

SECOND
THOUGHTS

PFERBS 19: 2